Selected Poems
of
Thomas Hardy

Selected Poems
of
Thomas Hardy

EDITED
AND WITH AN INTRODUCTION BY
JOHN CROWE RANSOM

COLLIER BOOKS
Macmillan Publishing Company
NEW YORK

Library of Congress catalog card number: 61-7054

First Collier Books Edition 1966

17   16   15   14   13   12   11   10

ISBN 0-02-070490-9

Poems from *Human Shows, Far Phantasies, Songs and Trifles* Copyright 1925 by Macmillan Publishing Co., Inc. Copyright renewed 1953 by Lloyds Bank Ltd. Poems from *Winter Words* Copyright 1928 by Florence E. Hardy and Sydney E. Cockerell; Copyright renewed 1927 by Lloyds Bank Ltd.

Macmillan Publishing Company
866 Third Avenue, New York, N.Y. 10022

Printed in the United States of America

CONTENTS

v

INTRODUCTION

By the end of the second decade of our century, we had become excited over the beginnings of several fresh kinds of American verse; we had the feeling that some spectacular advance was about to be made in our native literature. But in one way or another we came upon certain poems by Thomas Hardy which had nothing to do with the happy event, yet exhilarated us nevertheless. We responded with that "shock of recognition" by which we assent to some bold new verse as being, after all, within the canon of poetry. They moved some of us more deeply and longer than the pieces of our own nationals. Fresh as these little poems were, they were timeless in their grand manner. We knew that the old Victorian novelist had turned to poetry; perhaps we even knew that he had only turned back to his first and favored Muse. But we could not have foreseen the valor or the ingenuity of his imagination. It was a metaphysical imagination, in the service of a theological passion. In verse he could indulge directly and freely in speculations which he could only introduce in the Wessex novels as the author's gloss or digression, and we could see why he had felt obliged to change his Muses again. Certainly this verse was not in the fashion of any of the new poetries. In that stirring and revolutionary period of ours the elaborate but uniform stanzas of Hardy, descending their page so primly, looked slightly forbidding; and when we were reading them we may have been put off sometimes by a certain quaintness in their diction. But once the reader had engaged with them, the chances were that he would have to go on and adopt them.

Probably ten or a dozen of these small poems will have their regular place within the choice anthologies of modern verse; as compositions secured in some specially terse form of poetic economy which suited the peculiar verbal imagination of this poet. They are like quick but sure little dramas; or in their folkways they make us think of epics in miniature. But if we look for the genre which seems most likely to describe them we may call them fables. They offer natural images of the gods in action or, sometimes unfortunately, in inaction. The sharp and homely detail of the country naturalist in Hardy is not compromised by the presence of deity and his ministers; these are made to answer in his own language to the naturalist or his spokesman in the poem. The tone of the composition may be altogether grave and earnest. But fable is a self-confessed fiction by an independent thinker, therefore very free in its images. As if to allow in advance for the failure of human speculations, including his own, Hardy often gives them a sporting or rowdy turn which makes them comic in their irony.

We came upon "Channel Firing" for example. A young critic said the poem was about "Sabre Rattling," but this was badly in error. Hardy might have written a poem under that title, but instead of being the poem we have it would have been a rather rhetorical exercise under a figure at that time conventional for journalists and statesmen, and not quite real; whereas the actual title is about what Hardy heard with his own ears, and could imagine being heard by the animals and ghosts on the coast of Wessex. The time of composition is fixed precisely by the date line under the poem as "April 1914," which was just two months before the fateful assassination at Serajevo.

CHANNEL FIRING

That night your great guns, unawares,
Shook all our coffins as we lay,
And broke the chancel window-squares,
We thought it was the Judgment-day

And sat upright. While drearisome
Arose the howl of wakened hounds,
The mouse let fall the altar-crumb,
The worms drew back into the mounds,

The glebe cow drooled. Till God called, "No;
It's gunnery practice out at sea
Just as before you went below;
The world is as it used to be:

"All nations striving strong to make
Red war yet redder. Mad as hatters
They do no more for Christés sake
Than you who are helpless in such matters.

"That this is not the judgment-hour
For some of them's a blessed thing,
For if it were they'd have to scour
Hell's floor for so much threatening. . . .

"Ha, ha. It will be warmer when
I blow the trumpet (if indeed
I ever do; for you are men,
And rest eternal sorely need)."

So down we lay again. "I wonder,
Will the world ever saner be,"
Said one, "than when He sent us under
In our indifferent century!"

And many a skeleton shook his head.
"Instead of preaching forty year,"
My neighbor Parson Thirdly said,
"I wish I had stuck to pipes and beer."

Again the guns disturbed the hour,
Roaring their readiness to avenge,
As far inland as Stourton Tower,
And Camelot, and starlit Stonehenge.

April 1914

The speaker is one of the clerical ghosts inhabiting the church-
yard; who are among the countless ghosts peopling Hardy's verse,

talking with each other, or even slipping from their mounds to go and talk with their old friends yet living. What they talk about usually is the bliss of their perfect rest. Now the gunfire scares the beasts, and causes the ghosts to think the Judgment Day is come to spoil everything for them. But the deity here is particularly obliging in Hardy's free and easy version of the orthodox Christian God. He reassures them, and after some menacing asides against the bellicose sinners he suggests that he may even reconsider his scheme of a universal resurrection, which will be too painful for the good ghosts to bear. He may just let things go on as usual. His part in the poem reminds us of many Old Testament stories in which the Lord spoke to the faithful about his grand designs and complained of the incorrigible sinners who perverted them. The ghosts are relieved of their fears, though they feel professionally let down. And the guns resume, with a roar which reaches even to the ancient shrines of the region. The poem ends, and the poet-theologian has not found his triumphant theology which will overthrow the powers of evil. Yet there is a remarkable stylistic change: the last lines are the most lyrical. We have seen that combination before in poetic drama, and it would appear to be the peculiar "resolution" of many tragedies. Our expectations have been defeated, but we still insist on our moral universe; the roar of the guns prevails, but now it assaults the shrines without effect. The finest technical detail of the poem is in the forced stresses which the meter places upon the last syllables of the final words: starlít Stonehénge. The compound words do not lose their meaning, but it changes slightly in emphasis. Hardy would have known what the -henge of Stonehenge meant, for he was by taste a student of local antiquities, and by professional training an ecclesiastical architect; besides, he had the New English Dictionary on his shelf. The poet is playing upon a sacred name, and its handsome epithet too, as if to say there is still vitality in this quarter. The thing heard upon the air is evil, but the thing seen is the religious monument hung and illuminated beneath the stars.

One of the most perfected of the theological or fabulous poems has to do with a set of characters identified by the military title as "The Subalterns"; they are the junior officers who possess no initiative of their own but have only to carry out the orders of the High Command.

I

"Poor wanderer," said the leaden sky,
    "I fain would lighten thee,
But there are laws in force on high
    Which say it must not be."

II

—"I would not freeze thee, shorn one," cried
    The North, "knew I but how
To warm my breath, to slack my stride,
    But I am ruled as thou."

III

—"Tomorrow I attack thee, wight,"
    Said Sickness. "Yet I swear
I bear thy little ark no spite
    But am bid enter there."

IV

—"Come hither, Son," I heard Death say;
    "I did not will a grave
Should end thy pilgrimage today,
    But I too am a slave."

V

We smiled upon each other then,
    And life to me had less
Of that fell look it wore ere when
    They owned their passiveness.

Perhaps we can afford the time to notice the extremely clean and formal workmanship of Hardy's best poems, including by all means the fabulous ones. A poem could not wear a tidier *look* than this one. The stanzas are numbered consecutively in Roman capitals. At one period, having tried the numbers successfully, Hardy was disposed to number the stanzas of most of his poems, indifferently. But otherwise, as here, the numbers may be meant to indicate that pains have been taken to make the stanzas as equal as they can be and still be progressive in the argument; then the numbering would be the author's trademark, his way of certifying the composition as being of his best workmanship. We may look at this poem typographically without reading it; that is the first response we make to a poem since the introduction of the printed page, and one that we may be sure the author is going to make. The stanzas are typographically equal, even if we compare them line by line. But a closer look discloses small differences. Each of the first four stanzas has two sets of quotes which together enclose most of the type; the middle part between the quotes is evidently the identification of the speaker. But the identifications vary slightly in length and position, and the quoted parts vary accordingly. The final stanza has no quotes, and will be the narrative conclusion after all the speakers have finished. The ecclesiastical architect in Hardy must have liked to find the poem looking this way; he would have been familiar with the series of members precisely equal in weight and function, yet different individually, in a good structure of masonry.

Or we may attend to the oral effect of the poem, reading it aloud for its rhythm without bothering over the meaning except insofar as we respond involuntarily by making associations with certain emphatic clanging words which vaguely give us the area of the meaning. Readers in our time are rather deaf to the meters of poetry. But the rhythm of this one is powerful and familiar, and so insistent that it clamors to be set to a tune. So we say "ballad measure"; but on second thought, mindful of certain associations, we say, "No; it must be scored to the music of a Church hymn; which after all must have appropriated more verse of this measure than ballad did." The measure here is C. M. or Common Measure; Hardy would have known it very well from the many hymns he had sung as a youth. Their tunes lingered nostalgically in his mind even after he had lost his faith, and we find him writing poems about them. At any rate the scruple of good workmanship shows just as clearly in hymnology as in architecture; and in the visual and aural versions of a poem as in the meaningful.

But we come to the meaning, which is our major preoccupation, and Hardy's. And we quickly discover that there is heresy in this poem which is not suitable for being associated either with the Church hymnal or with the architecture of Christian churches. There are no churches, nor hymns, which will embody or publish Hardy's peculiar views.

Each of the four Subalterns has an errand to perform at the expense of an innocent creature. They appear in a progressively worsening series in which the last Subaltern is Death. Two of them are meteorological agents; the leaden sky which depresses the spirits, and the North which freezes with its wind. And two are physiological agents, the familiar processes called Sickness and Death. All the four are good poets. Leaden sky sets the pattern; he would lighten the wanderer if he could, but he must obey the laws in force on high; that is to say, he is a natural force who may not stray from his appointed nature. Each of the other Subalterns throws in an intimate phrase taken from the language of faith, to indicate how strange it is to have to victimize so good a creature. North is going to turn his blast upon one who is like a shorn lamb; he is thinking of the Christian proverb, "God tempers the wind to the shorn lamb." It does not hold here. Sickness is about to invade his victim's little ark, despite what has been said about the Covenant, the promise of security, which is supposed to go with it. And Death will end a "pilgrimage"; that was the pious figure under which this victim had ordered his life.

The poet as narrator has the final stanza, and is the best poet of the five. The four Subalterns may have observed him listening to them, and stood by for a moment in order to confront him; but it is left to the reader's imagination to suppose how the final meeting does actually come about. They have something to tell each other, and we have seen that they possess a common language, but now their eloquence is in another medium, a silent but not less effective medium. There is registered a single confederated smile of five likeminded souls; whereupon the poet tells us of his own small comfort, when "They owned their passiveness."

In the theological configuration of this poem several of Hardy's views are working. To start at the top, the Law-giver has instituted the laws for his creation, and that seems to have been final, for it does not appear to be his intention to intervene mercifully and miraculously in their execution. If we wish to bring Hardy's views as much as possible under some variant or other of orthodox Christian doctrine, he might seem to us here a sort of eighteenth century

Deist; but the term does not occur in Hardy's usage. Next, there is Nature; and Nature as the complex of natural forces must appear to Hardy, as to any other naturalist, as the effective agent of evil when the Subalterns come to execute the laws. On the other hand, there is the other aspect of Nature which is of great importance to the poet at the end, and makes life tolerable: where Nature has full sympathy with men and would deal kindly with them if only the curse permitted it. In other poems of Hardy's, Nature is personified as the general Mother, doing the best she can to bring her creatures to birth and care for them; that is only the extension of the spirit of the Subalterns, and of course it is a theologism to which a great many poets are given in one form or another. And finally, the poet-narrator is a man, therefore emphatically of a moral complexion. Like the biological evolutionists, Hardy was familiar with the notion that man was the one being in the universe attested indubitably as having the moral sense; this he might violate—there are some unspeakable villains in Hardy's tales and small dramas in verse—but he would know he was doing it. As a species, man is corrigible, though Hardy wasted no time speculating as to whether man is perfectible. Hardy himself was one of the kindliest of men—we will recollect that stanza of his admirable poem "Afterwards" where he expresses the modest hope that when he comes to die,

If I pass during some nocturnal blackness, mothy and warm,
    When the hedgehog travels furtively over the lawn,
One may say, "He strove that such innocent creatures should come to
    no harm,
    But he could do little for them, and now he is gone."

His compassion for hedgehogs is very like that of the Subalterns for men, but so is his final helplessness or "passiveness."

Another fine poem, not yet generally adopted by anthologists, is one written shortly after the first World War about Armistice Day; the title is, "And There Was a Great Calm." It is one of the noble war poems in our language, or any language. To give it special dignity, Hardy writes this one in iambic pentameters, and their effect is stately, but they flow easily enough to assimilate the intense homely phrase here and there which is part of this poet's character, and must have its place in the midst of the big rhetoric. And now we are at the Front, and hear the cry, "War is done!" The last three stanzas go as follows:

VII

Aye; all was hushed. The about-to-fire fired not,
The aimed-at moved away in trance-lipped song.
One checkless regiment slung a clinching shot
And turned. The Spirit of Irony smirked out, "What?
Spoil peradventures woven of Rage and Wrong?"

VIII

Thenceforth no flying fires inflamed the gray,
No hurtlings shook the dewdrop from the thorn,
No moan perplexed the mute bird on the spray;
Worn horses mused: "We are not whipped today";
No weft-winged engines blurred the moon's thin horn.

IX

Calm fell. From Heaven distilled a clemency;
There was peace on earth, and silence in the sky;
Some could, some could not, shake off misery:
The Sinister Spirit sneered, "It had to be!"
And again the Spirit of Pity whispered, "Why?"

Yet this is not the happy celebration it ought to be, when the right side has won. It is scarcely a happy ending at all. And again we hear Hardy's troubled Spirits talking: they have been borrowed without a bit of alteration from his own verse-drama, *The Dynasts*.

Hardy's Spirits have little rank or authority in the hierarchy of Heaven. They are planetary Spirits who hover over earth-events, and they have the moral intelligence of men, and the freedom to engage in interminable discussion of the manner in which events are directed by Heaven. We may not fancy, however, the smirk with which the Spirit of Irony asks, "Are they going to stop the show? And no more of these fortunes of battle?" Nor do we quite see why the Sinister Spirit has to sneer when he declares, "It had to be!" He is questioned by the Spirit of Pity in the last line but not refuted.

But Hardy is constitutionally so much under the domination of Pity, and so close to the event when he writes the Armistice poem, that he disparages the tone of the Spirit of Irony, and the tone of that Sinister Spirit who is the Spirit of Irony's identical twin, or the Spirit of Irony himself when we are not listening to him sympathetically; and forgets that Hardy the poet rates for us as decidedly the principal Voice of Irony among the poets of his age. We wish he might have wiped the smirk off the face of Irony, in that late line, and the sneer off the face of the Sinister Spirit, in that next-to-last line, in order to represent a great Spirit according to his honors.

Hardy's enormous verse-play offers such a reinforcement to the small fables that we must look backward briefly and bring it into our perspective. *The Dynasts* was designed by Hardy before he finished his career in fiction. The title-page gives accurate notice of its dimensions: *The Dynasts: an Epic-Drama of the War with Napoleon, in Three Parts, Nineteen Acts, and One Hundred and Thirty Scenes; the time covered by the action being about ten years.* The third and final Part appeared in 1908, when Hardy had advanced well into his second or poetic career. The work does not stand in his *Collected Poems* (which has volume enough with its more than 800 short poems), and passages excerpted from it do not invite inclusion in a *Selected Poems.* But its relation to the short poems written while it was under composition, and afterwards, is that of a powerful theological prepossession. Hardy knew the Greek drama, and Shelley's excellent adaptation of the form to his English version of *Prometheus Unbound;* Hardy greatly admired Shelley. He would have known Keats's poem *Hyperion,* which is Greek in its ideas but a highly lyrical narrative in form. So he proceeds to write a Greek drama of his own, following Shelley who followed Aeschylus, and following Keats who engaged with the common theme without following the usual genre. All the poets in this series are fabulists, and all are concerned with the notion of an evolution or refinement in the Greek godhead—like another refinement which figured a few centuries after the Greeks with another line of theologians and produced the Christian godhead. But Hardy's drama is a *tour de force,* being much the most difficult in execution, inasmuch as its action is not only historical, but modern. The Napoleonic wars were recent and fully documented; Hardy as a young man had known veterans who had fought in them. He could not do what Aristotle had commended the Greek playwrights for doing, that is to say, treat the actions and fortunes of the ancient houses, which the playwright could manipulate at will because they were legendary and antedated any sober historic annals. Nor could Hardy put gods into action on his stage. Like a scrupulous scholar he followed the naturalistic accounts, making bold dramatic manoeuvers in doing so. But he cast his drama in the Greek style in what was perhaps its crucial feature: he invented a fabulous company of Spirits congenial with his moods and ideas, to play the role of Chorus and make their incessant comment. The Spirit or Spirits of Pity are there, grieving because the Immanent Will which causes all events works unconsciously and without care for Its human creatures; but ready at any moment to exclaim rapturously that now at last It is beginning to rise into consciousness and compassion. The Spirit or Spirits of Irony are there too, where they can always reply to the Pities that there is yet no sure sign of the event. Incidentally, they seem to find a perverse pleasure in watching the show, remarking for example at one point in prose, "War makes rattling good history"; as if they attended upon a comic spectacle. It is from *The Dynasts* that the Spirit of Pity and the Spirit of Irony have moved into the Armistice Poem at the end of a war which has ended as the Napoleonic wars did, when the good side has triumphed, and when just as before it appears that

Some could, some could not, shake off misery.

In Irony there is surely a comic sense working; and a comic effect is a relief-mechanism. An ironic poem makes a great joke, and it is upon the poet and his readers, who take it gladly if their sensibilities are being harrowed. It parries the force of the tragic blow, at least partially; and momentarily, or better than that, for it may be stubborn enough to have a long life. The Spirit of Pity is strong in us, it *must* be justified in the event—but what a logical paradox is this for pondering, when suddenly the event is otherwise! The mind has to manage a very complicated economy. It is given to arranging its intellectual counters, which are its utilities, and its physical images, which are its pictures, as advantageously as possible; and is not prepared to abandon the plan of the house hastily when some of its furnitures appear suddenly to "clash" with the rest. For the human community lives as a matter of course, compulsively, under two flags, two sovereignties, and is not that a contradiction in terms? There is a natural order within which events go according to a natural law; we have acknowledged the law, and labored to understand it, and learned to use it often to our own advantage; we did not institute it. There is also a moral order, whose law is Justice and Pity; we mean to deal justly and charitably, and to enforce the law against our rebel members. But if the two laws clash, and the natural law prevails? We are always unprepared for that event. When it is most unexpected we wonder if the moral order is anything more than what we legislated into being, not absolute at all as a sovereignty must be, but choose not to concede the point at once, and are willing to seem slightly ridiculous if we must, while we think and wait. We say to ourselves, "It is incredible." And do not our memories hold the image of some scene where the final obsequies have been performed over the body of a good husband, and the chief mourner in her widow's weeds turns decently to say to her friends as if in self-defense, but half-hoping for confirmation, "You see I am not crying yet because I cannot. I am still unable to believe it." But what has been breached is not the mechanical logic of natural events, but the moral logic of justice to which Pity adheres. We are suspended irresolute in our choice between the universe of *ought to be* and the conflicting universe of *is*.

There is a Spirit beyond the Spirit of Irony, which we had best call the Classical Spirit. It is strong enough and wise enough to acknowledge the tragic event serenely because this bad luck has already been allowed for. Its faith is in a created world in which our species can manage very well because we are adapted biologically to it, and by acting rationally become better and better adapted. The Subalterns such as we can distinguish must execute its laws, but they are at least as beneficent as they are harsh. Though the final outcome for individual man is death, he has a good chance to realize his share of happiness; and this for him, peculiarly among the created forms of life, is conscious and thrilling precisely because of his sense of the perils by which it is invested. He feels that the world is good, perhaps that it is the best of all possible worlds, as the religious philosopher said; and when he thinks of its creator he would be theologically of some Deistic persuasion.

The Classical Spirit moves in any literature. Roman Horace possessed it magnificently, but so did Marvell, for example, in our own language; so did Shakespeare, and even Tennyson intermittently, in spite of his melancholy cast. But we are most familiar with this Spirit in Aristotle's version of Greek tragedy, where the unfolding drama stirs the Spirit of Pity, but then as the tragic event becomes more and more imminent we are overtaken by the Spirit of Fear. After the event we are purged and at peace again. Probably we wish to take a small exception here to Aristotle's Spirit of Fear. That would be a private and self-regarding affect, and it would hardly consist with the magnanimous Spirit of Pity at the same time. As Aristotle said, "Pity is occasioned by undeserved misfortune [happening to the tragic hero], and Fear by that of one like ourselves." We should hope that the pitying poet might obtain readers or auditors of his own unselfish kind; we would like to regard him as the champion of his struggling fellow-creatures, not playing his own game, and we would like to share if possible in his attitude. But Aristotle had in mind the un-literary and unprepared common Greek spectator, and for that purpose his account is right. Like a good modern psychologist he understands the tangle of motivations which move people commonly, and wants his artist to succeed even with the lower ones. So, in surviving the tragic ending, we the spectators find ourselves still here, and unharmed. The fear is purged away. Furthermore, we have not seen the stage emptied at the end, for new *personae* have appeared there, and new hopeful plans are being made against the future. The wisdom of the Classical Spirit probably consists in a strong pragmatic or empirical impression of the usual modes of bad fortune, and the rate and occasion of their incidence. The stroke has descended before our eyes, and conceivably it may aim next at ourselves; but that is not too likely according to the Classical Spirit, who may even have made statistical reckoning of the probability. Prometheus has long been delivered from his bonds, and has performed hugely for the race. He is a great actuary of the mortality tables; his ingenuity has taught us to predict the course of the Subalterns and evade them, or even sometimes so to arrange matters as to employ them in our own service.

The Spirit in which we enter into the tale or drama of the dangerous human adventure is always the Spirit of Pity, whose literary name is the Romantic Spirit. The faith of that Spirit amounts to an enthusiasm; the gods will fulfill the hero's innocent and natural undertaking, they have decreed fulfillment and success everywhere in the scheme of his life. But the Classical Spirit has observed that this does not quite appear to be the intention of Heaven. So as the play proceeds we have an over-drama of the progress of the spectator's soul from Pity to Horror, or from Pity to Fear to Purgation; from Pity to Irony, in Hardy's case, for a period of indecision; or best of all from Pity to the Classical Spirit, which accepts the distasteful event and prepares for whatever will come next.

But it is easy to see why Hardy's distress is heavy in the time of war. Then the destruction and suffering are on a scale which is abnormal. If we look for braggadocio in Hardy anywhere, it will be in his frequent intimation that, as for himself, he is quite ready for the grave. But this occurs when he is already old and tired. As for war, however: "In peace the sons bury their fathers, but in war the fathers bury their sons"; according to Herodotus, this was said by King Midas, who had listened to the wisdom of Solon. It is difficult even for the Classical Spirit to allow for that calamity, which endangers the survival of the species itself. When Hardy was composing *The Dynasts,* he felt there could not be another war so bad as the Napoleonic one, but he was mistaken; he had to live through the first of our World Wars. Fortunately for him, when he died in 1928, nobody particularly expected the second.

Many other writers are melancholic like Hardy, and sometimes they are ironic too. We may feel impelled by the title to read Doctor Johnson's "The Vanity of Human Wishes," but we will not find its irony consistent; we may feel impelled also to read Ecclesiastes the secular Preacher because of his refrain of "Vanity," but we will have to say that it is forced out of him involuntarily in spite of his piety, and that he scarcely knows the drift of what he is saying every now and then, as for example: "Consider the work of God: for who can make that straight, which he hath made crooked?"

But in one near quarter Hardy finds unexpected company. For there is Browning, the most prolix of poets, yet the one whose doctrine of Christian compassion seemed least to waver; his steadfastness was militant, like the archangel Michael's. At the age of twenty Browning had got published without any author's name the long poem called *Pauline;* he acknowledged his authorship when Dante Gabriel Rossetti, many years later, read the book in the British Museum and taxed him with it, on the ground of its style and sentiment. It is a youthful but noble poem. The speaker finds his hero first in Shelley, who had celebrated the deliverance of Prometheus the compassionate Spirit of Science. Then the poet had discovered Christ, who eclipsed even Shelley's expectations of Prometheus; and he tells of his wide theological studies, and his secure choice of Christ as the Hero he will preach. After that it was as if Browning gloried in finding evil, as if it only gave him the chance to declare instantly and roundly that evil was going to be vanquished. But when, and where? Hardy thought that Browning's optimism came too cheaply. But in 1889 he read that miscellany of poems bearing the title of *Asolando;* it was Browning's last book, issued on the day of his death. On the evidence of certain poems there Hardy felt that he had undervalued Browning as a thinker. For Browning had come to fear that "Power," by which he seemed to mean Power careless and brutal in its incidence, might be really too strong for Love or Pity to counter on this earth. What then? There is the strange little last poem, the "Epilogue to Asolando," in which Browning promises to carry on the fight in Heaven. When he shall come to die, Browning asks his friends not to think of him "At the midnight, in the silence of the sleep-time," nor as being in the grave "by death, fools think, imprisoned," but—

> No, at noonday in the bustle of man's work-time
>   Greet the unseen with a cheer!
> Bid him forward, breast and back as either should be,
> "Strive and thrive!" cry "Speed,—fight on, fare ever
>   There as here!"

Hardy must have relished this heresy. It is like Hardy's extremity of Irony: to find evil in Heaven. We have been instructed that Heaven is all goodness, but then we have been told also, by Plato and Scripture, that we shall be changed biologically before entering into that phase of the soul's existence. It is beyond our power to imagine the change; imagination being of the earth, earthy, like the five senses from which it always borrows. But Browning is taking the natural human predicament into Heaven, like Hardy, who thought it must be righted there.

How difficult it was for Hardy to manage his religious difficulties!

We think of him wishing he might return to the religious community of his boyhood, to the old faith, and the physical Church and its hymns. He was deterred, as many another naturalist must be more or less, by his conscientious objection to reciting the belief that God interposes in the execution of the natural laws by the faithful Subalterns. But he had the Spirit of Irony to mitigate his distress. The ironic disposition of evil may look to us like an interim arrangement, while he was collecting his wits and gathering his courage again; and so it was. Yet there is a massive but naughty pleasure in one's indecision when the choice is between two conflicting allegiances so momentous as Science and Faith, and naturally it can be prolonged. If deprived by some compunction of this refuge he would have had to embrace Science and go without Faith. But meanwhile it was as if he were holding in abeyance the processes of nature while he gave time to some transcendent order to assert itself. We understand the sequel; irony became his rule.

Most of Hardy's poems are naturalistic rather than fabulous and theological, and their ironies are commonplace. Sometimes the poems are fabulous or half-fabulous without being theological in any crucial or systematic fashion. And now we must try to come down gradually from the elevation of the excellent fables such as we have been discussing.

During the period of his poetry, Hardy thought of death as an abiding rest from the troubles of life; that was according to his years and his taste. But in the famous anthology piece, "Friends Beyond," this sense of death is uttered so defiantly that it seems to be in conscious refutation of Christian theology. Yet several times he offers another version of the state after death, and this one appears best in "Transformations." It is according to an ancient fancy which has its sweetness, and is not particularly concerned with its status as systematic theology. In this poem a number of bodies have been laid in the same plot, and their several survivals can be seen in the conformations of the yew-tree or other flora which the body's decay sustains. What is more, the poet knew that family group, and the differentiation of their personal forms seems to make for special authenticity.

TRANSFORMATIONS

Portion of this yew
Is a man my grandsire knew,
Bosomed here at its foot;
This branch may be his wife,
A ruddy human life
Now turned to a green shoot.

These grasses must be made
Of her who often prayed,
Last century, for repose;
And the fair girl long ago
Whom I often tried to know
May be entering this rose.

So, they are not underground,
But as veins and nerves abound
In the growths of upper air,
And they feel the sun and rain,
And the energy again
That made them what they were!

And we should look at one of many poems addressed to his dead first wife; she was the woman who "opened the door of the West to me," and "opened the door of Romance to me," the woman he had seen riding on the Western cliffs over the sea, and married in 1870. Immediately after her death in 1912 he had written a group of poems in her memory, and he continued to write them after he had married his faithful secretary in 1914. In this one he has no hesitation in adopting, for their joint purpose, her own Scriptural theology. He imagines their meeting in the afterworld, though in a dismal place, to accomplish one fine thing that he had neglected to bring about during her lifetime. They must sing together a tune they both had loved.

ON THE TUNE CALLED THE
OLD-HUNDRED-AND-FOURTH

We never sang together
    Ravenscroft's terse old tune
On Sundays or on weekdays,
In sharp or sunny weather,
    At night-time or at noon.

Why did we never sing it,
    Why never so incline
On Sundays or on weekdays,
Even when soft wafts would wing it
    From your far floor to mine?

Shall we that tune, then, never
    Stand voicing side by side
On Sundays or on weekdays? . . .
Or shall we, when for ever
    In Sheol we abide,

Sing it in desolation,
    As we might long have done
On Sundays or on weekdays
With love and exultation
    Before our sands had run?

One poem pictures a happy family doing very well in the world, but each of the four stanzas has for pendant a refrain of two lines which utters an ironic vision of the ruin to come. We may suppose they are spoken by the poet, who perhaps has been reading a series of gay letters from his friends, but since the weather is bad where he is, inside as well as outside his head, he cannot keep down his own constitutional misgivings. But perhaps the refrain-parts are fabulous, as coming from some Cassandra, singing of the doom to come though nobody would believe her. Or are they rendered by a Chorus of Pities and Ironies, commenting in unison a piece of domestic history?

DURING WIND AND RAIN

They sing their dearest songs—
He, she, all of them—yea,
Treble and tenor and bass,
 And one to play;
With the candles mooning each face. . . .
 Ah, no; the years O!
How the sick leaves reel down in throngs!

They clear the creeping moss—
Elders and juniors—aye,
Making the pathways neat
 And the garden gay;
And they build a shady seat. . . .
 Ah, no; the years, the years;
See, the white storm-birds wing across!

They are blithely breakfasting all—
Men and maidens—yea,
Under the summer tree,
 With a glimpse of the bay,
While pet fowl come to the knee. . . .
 Ah, no; the years O!
And the rotten rose is ript from the wall.

They change to a high new house,
He, she, all of them—aye,
Clocks and carpets, and chairs
 On the lawn all day,
And brightest things that are theirs. . . .
 Ah, no; the years, the years;
Down their carved names the rain-drop ploughs.

And sometimes there are poems of rare quality which fail of perfection. In the following one we are within sight of an exquisite thing which aspired and did not fall short; we have the sense of a new gallantry within the range of a domestic poetry. Yet we know that the beauty is faulted.

WIVES IN THE SERE

I

Never a careworn wife but shows,
     If a joy suffuse her,
Something beautiful to those
     Patient to peruse her,
Some one charm the world unknows,
     Precious to a muser,
Haply what, ere years were foes,
     Moved her mate to choose her.

II

But, be it a hint of rose
     That an instant hues her,
Or some early light or pose
     Wherewith thought renews her—
Seen by him at full, ere woes
     Practised to abuse her—
Sparely comes it, quickly goes,
     Time again subdues her.

Logically the stanzas are two, but so far as the rhyme-system goes they might as well be one. The eight odd-numbered lines of the poem rhyme together in a masculine ending, and the eight even-numbered lines rhyme in a feminine ending. The feminine rhymes are not very choice. *Muser* is probably the base, and it will do very well, but all the companion rhymes must manage with a verbal suffix followed by a *her,* as in suf-*fuse her;* and we are uncomfortable over that silent *h,* and the over-latinity which makes this diction too ponderous for the grace of the occasion. It was pedantic of Hardy to try for technical success by forcing his native language to such rude measures. But the delicacy of his intention is apparent, and we are grateful.

On the whole, the common or naturalistic verse of Hardy is uneven in its merits, and only now and then of high distinction. Fable stimulates Hardy both philosophically and verbally, and even a little of fable entering into the natural action can make a great difference, as we have seen. But elsewhere? Perhaps we may generalize without too much risk about two kinds of composition which produce a vast number of the poems. First, there are the tales which are more or less on the order of the folk-ballads. Almost always in these the tragic story is racy and bold in its conception, and told in good order, but lacks that vividness, and finality of phrase, that we want most desperately. And we feel like saying that Hardy knew the behaviors of the folk, and knew their diction too, so far as his comic purposes were concerned—see "The Ruined Maid" for example—but did not know how they could make the diction tragic nor how they could make it poetic. That would be the well-kept secret of the old oral or anonymous ballads. Few of the lettered poets have known that secret. Wordsworth did not possess it.

Next, more of the poems than we would suspect, among those of an occasional or incidental sort, are autobiographical; and if we do not know the personal history behind them, they are likely to seem too brief and scanty in their development. It is remarkable what a difference is made in our reception if we know the actual context of these poems as Hardy did; or as his widow Florence Hardy knew them for example, and as she tells us about them in her writings. Hardy himself will tell us less than the whole significant truth, and it is hardly enough. And as a matter of fact critics have long made a grievance of that sort of thing, and sometimes advised writers not to use true stories for their prose fictions. But they might especially advise poets to this effect. Hardy does not fail particularly in developing his narratives; it is in the odd and occasional poems that he is too terse for our understanding—and too autobiographical.

Close comparative testing is always being done by anthologists and other curious readers within the huge collection of Hardy's poems. Rarely do two of them come out with anything like the same list of poems chosen; though each when he studies the other's list is likely to be struck with the sense of its equal justice. Probably there are few happy hunting grounds which can be explored as long as Hardy's verse by literary collectors looking for specimens. Some of the very good ones take a lot of finding, and much painstaking evaluation.

And when nothing else in the landscape seems to demand their attention, there is always the forbidding thicket of the *Satires of*

Circumstance; that is the title of the fifteen numbered little poems as a group, and of the big book of 1914 which includes them. They have a dozen or two lines each, being given to maximum economy without loss of perfect clarity; they are in nondescript meters, and run to horrid endings. They must be taken in the comic sense which is intended. They are satires rather than proper tragedies, being poems in which the victims are not entitled to our sympathy. The joke is upon persons who have to be punished because they were foolish; because they were more innocent than anybody can afford to be in this world. The qualified reader is one who is able as he reads to recover his sophistication quickly if he had the least inclination to be sympathetic. Hardy means to try the propriety of our responses. And this time there are no Subalterns to execute the sentence in obedience to Heaven; but members of the victims' own kind, with cruelties and treacheries peculiarly human, and made possible because the victims have exposed themselves where they were most vulnerable, being infatuated or vain and self-righteous. The Satires represent Hardy about mid-point of his poetic career in a mood of ferocity which we might hardly have expected. He enlarges himself for us in respect of his psychic capabilities, though the gentle reader may not like him any the better. The Satires have made some entry by now into the anthologies. Let us notice No. XIV, which is less lurid than most in its surprise, but is likely to linger longer in our minds, and make some disturbance within our conventional mores.

OVER THE COFFIN

They stand confronting, the coffin between,
His wife of old, and his wife of late,
And the dead man whose they both had been
Seems listening aloof, as to things past date.
—"I have called," says the first. "Do you marvel or not?"
"In truth," says the second, "I do—somewhat."

"Well, there was a word to be said by me! . . .
I divorced that man because of you—
It seemed I must do it, boundenly;

But now I am older, and tell you true,
For life is little, and dead lies he;
I would I had let alone you two!
And both of us, scorning parochial ways,
Had lived like the wives in the patriarchs' days."

The 125 poems which follow are taken from the *Collected Poems,* except the last two, which are out of *Winter Words*—the posthumous publication from a manuscript which Hardy had not yet released. The order is that of the *Collected Poems,* which follows the order of publication of the single volumes. The date which Hardy often appends to a poem indicates that it does not belong chronologically to the volume in which it appears; such dates are retained in the present selection wherever they seem necessary for the understanding of readers who do not possess the collected edition. Only two or three slight footnotes by the editor have seemed to be called for.

In conclusion let us set the poet securely but very simply in the historical perspective of English verse. Let us say that Hardy is the third Victorian poet, after Tennyson and Browning.

Nevertheless, some dates must be duly noticed. Tennyson lived from 1809 to 1892, Browning from 1812 to 1889, Hardy from 1840 to 1928; and Victoria's reign lasted from 1837 to 1901. Each poet attained to a very great age. But Tennyson and Browning had found their own true voices and matured by the time Victoria came to the throne; they advanced the careers which they had launched, and did not survive her. Hardy's published verse starts in 1865; the first three poems in our selection are of 1866 and 1867. But much the larger fraction of the whole of his verse was written after the Victorian period had come to its official end. How may we refer to Hardy as a Victorian poet simply and without qualification?

We will leave for a moment the difficulty of the dates, and review a little biography. Hardy was trained as an ecclesiastical architect, and in the early sixties he had left Dorset and was in London under professional employment. But that was the great decade of the age, intellectually speaking. The Faith of England came under attack from two quarters at once, and good churchmen did not fail to respond with fury. The enemies were first the Darwinians, of course, following upon the publication of *The Origin of Species* in 1859; and then the proponents of that "Higher Criticism" of the Scriptures which after a sufficient lag had arrived from the Continent, and gained English adherents in pulpit and university. The young Hardy in London was bound to attend closely upon the clamor of both disputations. He proceeded presently to lose the faith in which he had been nurtured; then to enter upon literature—perhaps most immediately in order to confirm and publish his own theological speculations. He tried verse, which was his natural medium, but could not find a market; before long he was engaged upon prose fiction, and met with better success; he did not leave this field till the nineties, when he had completed the prodigious Wessex novels. Turning back to verse, he began where he had left off, and published in 1898 his first book of poems, called *Wessex Poems and Other Verses*.

The "Wessex" poems are Victorian work by any standards. But they are not different from their companions, the "Other" and earlier verses, in their rebellious theology, nor in their quaint but original diction. Nor do the poems of later volumes which are post-Victorian in date differ substantially from them in either respect, but only in the wealth of their fresh occasions and forms. The poet's art advances but the poet does not change his habit; and for example he never intimates any interest in the very different poetry being written in the new century, though he lives into and past its first quarter. Hardy knew what his theme must be, and even his tone and idiom; his mind had enclosed its whole project, tentacularly. This was a man of character.

It has often been remarked that Hardy is close to the succeeding generation of poets and readers by reason of his naturalism and rebellion against the dogma. And if he never rested in his search for the Unknown God, that is not uniquely a sign of the fallen Victorian, for there are many recent and living poets to whom we must attribute this history; indeed it may be attributed with some confidence to almost any serious poet.

So it seems possible to say rather easily, and with substantial if not chronological accuracy, what is Hardy's place in English letters. Tennyson and Browning are orthodox in their piety, and we will say they are early Victorian poets; if Tennyson's orthodoxy sometimes wavers, it is not enough to keep him from being Poet Laureate. But

Hardy is a disaffected religionist, and we will say he is a late Victorian poet. The age which we style Victorian is not quite so sure and pure as many of its critics have wished to think; it is entitled to a major poet with something like the modern temper. Hardy is that poet, and the age becomes more reputable for having him.

JOHN CROWE RANSOM

Selected Poems
of
Thomas Hardy

HAP

If but some vengeful god would call to me
From up the sky, and laugh: "Thou suffering thing,
Know that thy sorrow is my ecstasy,
That thy love's loss is my hate's profiting!"

Then would I bear it, clench myself, and die,
Steeled by the sense of ire unmerited;
Half-eased in that a Powerfuller than I
Had willed and meted me the tears I shed.

But not so. How arrives it joy lies slain,
And why unblooms the best hope ever sown?
—Crass Casualty obstructs the sun and rain,
And dicing Time for gladness casts a moan. . . .
These purblind Doomsters had as readily strown
Blisses about my pilgrimage as pain.

1866.

A CONFESSION TO A FRIEND IN TROUBLE

Your troubles shrink not, though I feel them less
Here, far away, than when I tarried near;
I even smile old smiles—with listlessness—
Yet smiles they are, not ghastly mockeries mere.

A thought too strange to house within my brain
Haunting its outer precincts I discern:
—*That I will not show zeal again to learn*
Your griefs, and, sharing them, renew my pain. . . .

It goes, like murky bird or buccaneer
That shapes its lawless figure on the main,
And staunchness tends to banish utterly
The unseemly instinct that had lodgment here;

Yet, comrade old, can bitterer knowledge be
Than that, though banned, such instinct was in me!

1866.

NEUTRAL TONES

We stood by a pond that winter day,
And the sun was white, as though chidden of God,
And a few leaves lay on the starving sod;
    —They had fallen from an ash, and were gray.

Your eyes on me were as eyes that rove
Over tedious riddles of years ago;
And some words played between us to and fro
    On which lost the more by our love.

The smile on your mouth was the deadest thing
Alive enough to have strength to die;
And a grin of bitterness swept thereby
    Like an ominous bird a-wing. . . .

Since then, keen lessons that love deceives,
And wrings with wrong, have shaped to me
Your face, and the God-curst sun, and a tree,
    And a pond edged with grayish leaves.

1867.

FRIENDS BEYOND

William Dewy, Tranter Reuben, Farmer Ledlow late at plough,
    Robert's kin, and John's, and Ned's,
And the Squire, and Lady Susan, lie in Mellstock churchyard now!

"Gone," I call them, gone for good, that group of local hearts and
       heads;
      Yet at mothy curfew-tide,
And at midnight when the noon-heat breathes it back from walls
      and leads,

They've a way of whispering to me—fellow-wight who yet abide—
      In the muted, measured note
Of a ripple under archways, or a lone cave's stillicide:

"We have triumphed: this achievement turns the bane to antidote,
      Unsuccesses to success,
Many thought-worn eves and morrows to a morrow free of thought.

"No more need we corn and clothing, feel of old terrestial stress;
      Chill detraction stirs no sigh;
Fear of death has even bygone us: death gave all that we possess."

W.D.—"Ye mid burn the old bass-viol that I set such value by."
Squire.—"You may hold the manse in fee,
      You may wed my spouse, may let my children's memory of me
      die."

Lady S.—"You may have my rich brocades, my laces; take each
      household key;
      Ransack coffer, desk, bureau;
      Quiz the few poor treasures hid there, con the letters kept by
      me."

Far.—"Ye mid zell my favourite heifer, ye mid let the charlock grow,
      Foul the grinterns, give up thrift."
Far. Wife—"If ye break my best blue china, children, I shan't care
      or ho."

All.—"We've no wish to hear the tidings, how the people's fortunes
      shift;
      What your daily doings are;
      Who are wedded, born, divided; if your lives beat slow or swift.

3

"Curious not the least are we if our intents you make or mar,
        If you quire to our old tune,
If the City stage still passes, if the weirs still roar afar."

—Thus, with very gods' composure, freed those crosses late and soon
        Which, in life, the Trine allow
(Why, none witteth), and ignoring all that haps beneath the moon.

William Dewy, Tranter Reuben, Farmer Ledlow late at plough,
        Robert's kin, and John's, and Ned's,
And the Squire, and Lady Susan, murmur mildly to me now.

NATURE'S QUESTIONING

When I look forth at dawning, pool,
        Field, flock, and lonely tree,
        All seem to gaze at me
Like chastened children sitting silent in a school;

        Their faces dulled, constrained, and worn,
        As though the master's ways
        Through the long teaching days
Had cowed them till their early zest was overborne.

        Upon them stirs in lippings mere
        (As if once clear in call,
        But now scarce breathed at all)—
"We wonder, ever wonder, why we find us here!

        "Has some Vast Imbecility,
        Mighty to build and blend,
        But impotent to tend,
Framed us in jest, and left us now to hazardry?

        "Or come we of an Automaton
        Unconscious of our pains? . . .

4

Or are we live remains
Of Godhead dying downwards, brain and eye now gone?

"Or is it that some high Plan betides,
        As yet not understood,
        Of Evil stormed by Good,
We the Forlorn Hope over which Achievement strides?"

Thus things around. No answerer I. . . .
        Meanwhile the winds, and rains,
        And Earth's old glooms and pains
Are still the same, and Life and Death are neighbours nigh.

THE IMPERCIPIENT

(AT A CATHEDRAL SERVICE)

That with this bright believing band
        I have no claim to be,
That faiths by which my comrades stand
        Seem fantasies to me,
And mirage-mists their Shining Land,
        Is a strange destiny.

Why thus my soul should be consigned
        To infelicity,
Why always I must feel as blind
        To sights my brethren see,
Why joys they've found I cannot find,
        Abides a mystery.

Since heart of mine knows not that ease
        Which they know; since it be
That He who breathes All's Well to these
        Breathes no All's-Well to me,
My lack might move their sympathies
        And Christian charity!

5

I am like a gazer who should mark
    An inland company
Standing upfingered, with "Hark! hark!
    The glorious distant sea!"
And feel, "Alas, 'tis but yon dark
    And wind-swept pine to me!"

Yet I would bear my shortcomings
    With meet tranquillity,
But for the charge that blessed things
    I'd liefer not have be.
O, doth a bird deprived of wings
    Go earth-bound wilfully!

  .   .   .   .   .

Enough. As yet disquiet clings
    About us. Rest shall we.

HEIRESS AND ARCHITECT

FOR A. W. BLOMFIELD

She sought the Studios, beckoning to her side
An arch-designer, for she planned to build.
He was of wise contrivance, deeply skilled
In every intervolve of high and wide—
    Well fit to be her guide.

    "Whatever it be,"
    Responded he,
With cold, clear voice, and cold, clear view,
"In true accord with prudent fashionings
For such vicissitudes as living brings,
And thwarting not the law of stable things,
    That will I do."

6

"Shape me," she said, "high halls with tracery
And open ogive-work, that scent and hue
Of buds, and travelling bees, may come in through,
The note of birds, and singings of the sea,
    For these are much to me."

        "An idle whim!"
        Broke forth from him
Whom nought could warm to gallantries:
"Cede all these buds and birds, the zephyr's call,
And scents, and hues, and things that falter all,
And choose as best the close and surly wall,
        For winters freeze."

"Then frame," she cried, "wide fronts of crystal glass,
That I may show my laughter and my light—
Light like the sun's by day, the stars' by night—
Till rival heart-queens, envying, wail, 'Alas,
    Her glory!' as they pass."

        "O maid misled!"
        He sternly said
Whose facile foresight pierced her dire;
"Where shall abide the soul when, sick of glee,
It shrinks, and hides, and prays no eye may see?
Those house them best who house for secrecy,
        For you will tire."

"A little chamber, then, with swan and dove
Ranged thickly, and engrailed with rare device
Of reds and purples, for a Paradise
Wherein my Love may greet me, I my Love,
    When he shall know thereof?"

        "This, too, is ill,"
        He answered still,
The man who swayed her like a shade.
"An hour will come when sight of such sweet nook

Would bring a bitterness too sharp to brook,
When brighter eyes have won away his look;
    For you will fade."

Then said she faintly: "O, contrive some way—
Some narrow winding turret, quite mine own,
To reach a loft where I may grieve alone!
It is a slight thing; hence do not, I pray,
    This last dear fancy slay!"

    "Such winding ways
    Fit not your days,"
Said he, the man of measuring eye;
"I must even fashion as the rule declares,
To wit: Give space (since life ends unawares)
To hale a coffined corpse adown the stairs;
    For you will die."

"I LOOK INTO MY GLASS"

I look into my glass,
And view my wasting skin,
And say, "Would God it came to pass
My heart had shrunk as thin!"

For then, I, undistrest
By hearts grown cold to me,
Could lonely wait my endless rest
With equanimity.

But Time, to make me grieve,
Part steals, lets part abide;
And shakes this fragile frame at eve
With throbbings of noontide.

THE SOULS OF THE SLAIN

I

The thick lids of Night closed upon me
Alone at the Bill
Of the Isle by the Race [1]—
Many-caverned, bald, wrinkled of face—
And with darkness and silence the spirit was on me
To brood and be still.

II

No wind fanned the flats of the ocean,
Or promontory sides,
Or the ooze by the strand,
Or the bent-bearded slope of the land,
Whose base took its rest amid everlong motion
Of criss-crossing tides.

III

Soon from out of the Southward seemed nearing
A whirr, as of wings
Waved by mighty-vanned flies,
Or by night-moths of measureless size,
And in softness and smoothness well-nigh beyond hearing
Of corporal things.

IV

And they bore to the bluff, and alighted—
A dim-discerned train
Of sprites without mould,
Frameless souls none might touch or might hold—
On the ledge by the turreted lantern, far-sighted
By men of the main.

[1] The "Race" is the turbulent sea-area off the Bill of Portland, where contrary tides meet.

V

And I heard them say "Home!" and I knew them
 For souls of the felled
 On the earth's nether bord
Under Capricorn, whither they'd warred,
And I neared in my awe, and gave heedfulness to them
 With breathings inheld.

VI

Then, it seemed, there approached from the northward
 A senior soul-flame
 Of the like filmy hue:
And he met them and spake: "Is it you,
O my men?" Said they, "Aye! We bear homeward and
  hearthward
 To feast on our fame!"

VII

"I've flown there before you," he said then:
 "Your households are well;
 But—your kin linger less
On your glory and war-mightiness
Than on dearer things."—"Dearer?" cried these from the
  dead then,
 "Of what do they tell?"

VIII

"Some mothers muse sadly, and murmur
 Your doings as boys—
 Recall the quaint ways
Of your babyhood's innocent days.
Some pray that, ere dying, your faith had grown firmer,
 And higher your joys.

IX

"A father broods: 'Would I had set him
 To some humble trade,
 And so slacked his high fire,
And his passionate martial desire;

And told him no stories to woo him and whet him
    To this dire crusade!"

X

"And, General, how hold out our sweethearts,
    Sworn loyal as doves?"
    —"Many mourn; many think
It is not unattractive to prink
Them in sables for heroes. Some fickle and fleet hearts
    Have found them new loves."

XI

"And our wives?" quoth another resignedly,
    "Dwell they on our deeds?"
    —"Deeds of home; that live yet
Fresh as new—deeds of fondness or fret;
Ancient words that were kindly expressed or unkindly,
    These, these have their heeds."

XII

—"Alas! then it seems that our glory
    Weighs less in their thought
    Than our old homely acts,
And the long-ago commonplace facts
Of our lives—held by us as scarce part of our story,
    And rated as nought!"

XIII

Then bitterly some: "Was it wise now
    To raise the tomb-door
    For such knowledge? Away!"
But the rest: "Fame we prized till to-day;
Yet that hearts keep us green for old kindness we prize now
    A thousand times more!"

XIV

Thus speaking, the trooped apparitions
    Began to disband
    And resolve them in two:

Those whose record was lovely and true
Bore to northward for home: those of bitter traditions
        Again left the land,

XV

And, towering to seaward in legions,
        They paused at a spot
        Overbending the Race—
That engulphing, ghast, sinister place—
Whither headlong they plunged, to the fathomless regions
        Of myriads forgot.

XVI

And the spirits of those who were homing
        Passed on, rushingly,
        Like the Pentecost Wind;
And the whirr of their wayfaring thinned
And surceased on the sky, and but left in the gloaming
        Sea-mutterings and me.

December 1899.

ROME: ON THE PALATINE

(*April* 1887)

We walked where Victor Jove was shrined awhile,
And passed to Livia's rich red mural show,
Whence, thridding cave and Criptoportico,
We gained Caligula's dissolving pile.

And each ranked ruin tended to beguile
The outer sense, and shape itself as though
It wore its marble gleams, its pristine glow
Of scenic frieze and pompous peristyle.

When lo, swift hands, on strings nigh overhead,
Began to melodize a waltz by Strauss:
It stirred me as I stood, in Cæsar's house,
Raised the old routs Imperial lyres had led,

And blended pulsing life with lives long done,
Till Time seemed fiction, Past and Present one.

ROME

AT THE PYRAMID OF CESTIUS NEAR THE
GRAVES OF SHELLEY AND KEATS

(1887)

Who, then, was Cestius,
And what is he to me?—
Amid thick thoughts and memories multitudinous
One thought alone brings he.

I can recall no word
Of anything he did;
For me he is a man who died and was interred
To leave a pyramid

Whose purpose was exprest
Not with its first design,
Nor till, far down in Time, beside it found their rest
Two countrymen of mine.

Cestius in life, maybe,
Slew, breathed out threatening;
I know not. This I know: in death all silently
He does a finer thing,

In beckoning pilgrim feet
With marble finger high

To where, by shadowy wall and history-haunted street,
    Those matchless singers lie. . . .

    —Say, then, he lived and died
    That stones which bear his name
Should mark, through Time, where two immortal Shades abide;
    It is an ample fame.

AT A LUNAR ECLIPSE

Thy shadow, Earth, from Pole to Central Sea,
Now steals along upon the Moon's meek shine
In even monochrome and curving line
Of imperturbable serenity.

How shall I link such sun-cast symmetry
With the torn troubled form I know as thine,
That profile, placid as a brow divine,
With continents of moil and misery?

And can immense Mortality but throw
So small a shade, and Heaven's high human scheme
Be hemmed within the coasts yon arc implies?

Is such the stellar gauge of earthly show,
Nation at war with nation, brains that teem,
Heroes, and women fairer than the skies?

TO LIFE

    O Life with the sad seared face,
      I weary of seeing thee,
And thy draggled cloak, and thy hobbling pace,
      And thy too-forced pleasantry!

I know what thou would'st tell
Of Death, Time, Destiny—
I have known it long, and know, too, well
What it all means for me.

But canst thou not array
Thyself in rare disguise,
And feign like truth, for one mad day,
That Earth is Paradise?

I'll tune me to the mood,
And mumm with thee till eve;
And maybe what as interlude
I feign, I shall believe!

DOOM AND SHE

I

There dwells a mighty pair—
Slow, statuesque, intense—
Amid the vague Immense:
None can their chronicle declare,
Nor why they be, nor whence.

II

Mother of all things made,
Matchless in artistry,
Unlit with sight is she.—
And though her ever well-obeyed
Vacant of feeling he.

III

The Matron mildly asks—
A throb in every word—
"Our clay-made creatures, lord,
How fare they in their mortal tasks
Upon Earth's bounded bord?

IV

"The fate of those I bear,
Dear lord, pray turn and view,
And notify me true;
Shapings that eyelessly I dare
Maybe I would undo.

V

"Sometimes from lairs of life
Methinks I catch a groan,
Or multitudinous moan,
As though I had schemed a world of strife,
Working by touch alone."

VI

"World-weaver!" he replies,
"I scan all thy domain;
But since nor joy nor pain
It lies in me to recognize,
Thy questionings are vain."

VII

"World-weaver! what *is* Grief?
And what are Right, and Wrong,
And Feeling, that belong
To creatures all who owe thee fief?
Why is Weak worse than Strong?" . . .

VIII

—Unanswered, curious, meek,
She broods in sad surmise. . . .
—Some say they have heard her sighs
On Alpine height or Polar peak
When the night tempests rise.

THE SUBALTERNS

I

"Poor wanderer," said the leaden sky,
    "I fain would lighten thee,
But there are laws in force on high
    Which say it must not be."

II

—"I would not freeze thee, shorn one," cried
    The North, "knew I but how
To warm my breath, to slack my stride;
    But I am ruled as thou."

III

—"To-morrow I attack thee, wight,"
    Said Sickness. "Yet I swear
I bear thy little ark no spite,
    But am bid enter there."

IV

—"Come hither, Son," I heard Death say;
    "I did not will a grave
Should end thy pilgrimage to-day,
    But I, too, am a slave!"

V

We smiled upon each other then,
    And life to me had less
Of that fell look it wore ere when
    They owned their passiveness.

GOD-FORGOTTEN

I towered far, and lo! I stood within
The presence of the Lord Most High,

Sent thither by the sons of Earth, to win
    Some answer to their cry.

—"The Earth, sayest thou? The Human race?
By Me created? Sad its lot?
Nay: I have no remembrance of such place:
    Such world I fashioned not."—

—"O Lord, forgive me when I say
Thou spakest the word that made it all."—
"The Earth of men—let me bethink me. . . . Yea!
    I dimly do recall

"Some tiny sphere I built long back
(Mid millions of such shapes of mine)
So named. . . . It perished, surely—not a wrack
    Remaining, or a sign?

"It lost my interest from the first,
My aims therefor succeeding ill;
Haply it died of doing as it durst?"—
    "Lord, it existeth still."—

"Dark, then, its life! For not a cry
Of aught it bears do I now hear;
Of its own act the threads were snapt whereby
    Its plaints had reached mine ear.

"It used to ask for gifts of good,
Till came its severance, self-entailed,
When sudden silence on that side ensued,
    And has till now prevailed.

"All other orbs have kept in touch;
Their voicings reach me speedily:
Thy people took upon them overmuch
    In sundering them from me!

"And it is strange—though sad enough—
Earth's race should think that one whose call
Frames, daily, shining spheres of flawless stuff
Must heed their tainted ball! . . .

"But sayest it is by pangs distraught,
And strife, and silent suffering?—
Sore grieved am I that injury should be wrought
Even on so poor a thing!

"Thou shouldst have learnt that *Not to Mend*
For Me could mean but *Not to Know:*
Hence, Messengers! and straightway put an end
To what men undergo." . . .

Homing at dawn, I thought to see
One of the Messengers standing by.
—Oh, childish thought! . . . Yet often it comes to me
When trouble hovers nigh.

BY THE EARTH'S CORPSE

I

"O Lord, why grievest Thou?—
Since Life has ceased to be
Upon this globe, now cold
As lunar land and sea,
And humankind, and fowl, and fur
Are gone eternally,
All is the same to Thee as ere
They knew mortality."

II

"O Time," replied the Lord,
"Thou readest me ill, I ween;
Were all *the same*, I should not grieve

At that late earthly scene,
Now blestly past—though planned by me
With interest close and keen!—
Nay, nay: things now are *not* the same
As they have earlier been.

III

"Written indelibly
On my eternal mind
Are all the wrongs endured
By Earth's poor patient kind,
Which my too oft unconscious hand
Let enter undesigned.
No god can cancel deeds foredone,
Or thy old coils unwind!

IV

"As when, in Noë's days,
I whelmed the plains with sea,
So at this last, when flesh
And herb but fossils be,
And, all extinct, their piteous dust
Revolves obliviously,
That I made Earth, and life, and man,
It still repenteth me!"

TO LIZBIE BROWNE

I

Dear Lizbie Browne,
Where are you now?
In sun, in rain?—
Or is your brow
Past joy, past pain,
Dear Lizbie Browne?

II

Sweet Lizbie Browne
How you could smile,
How you could sing!—
How archly wile
In glance-giving,
Sweet Lizbie Browne!

III

And, Lizbie Browne,
Who else had hair
Bay-red as yours,
Or flesh so fair
Bred out of doors,
Sweet Lizbie Browne?

IV

When, Lizbie Browne,
You had just begun
To be endeared
By stealth to one,
You disappeared
My Lizbie Browne!

V

Ay, Lizbie Browne,
So swift your life,
And mine so slow,
You were a wife
Ere I could show
Love, Lizbie Browne.

VI

Still, Lizbie Browne,
You won, they said,
The best of men
When you were wed. . . .

Where went you then,
O Lizbie Browne?

VII

Dear Lizbie Browne,
I should have thought,
"Girls ripen fast,"
And coaxed and caught
You ere you passed,
Dear Lizbie Browne!

VIII

But, Lizbie Browne,
I let you slip;
Shaped not a sign;
Touched never your lip
With lip of mine,
Lost Lizbie Browne!

IX

So, Lizbie Browne,
When on a day
Men speak of me
As not, you'll say,
"And who was he?"—
Yes, Lizbie Browne!

"I NEED NOT GO"

I need not go
Through sleet and snow
To where I know
She waits for me;
She will tarry me there
Till I find it fair,
And have time to spare
From company.

When I've overgot
The world somewhat,
When things cost not
Such stress and strain,
Is soon enough
By cypress sough
To tell my Love
I am come again.

And if some day,
When none cries nay,
I still delay
To seek her side,
(Though ample measure
Of fitting leisure
Await my pleasure)
She will not chide.

What—not upbraid me
That I delayed me,
Nor ask what stayed me
So long? Ah, no!—
New cares may claim me,

New cares may claim me,
New loves inflame me,
She will not blame me,
But suffer it so.

HIS IMMORTALITY

I

I saw a dead man's finer part
Shining within each faithful heart
Of those bereft. Then said I: "This must be
    His immortality."

II

I looked there as the seasons wore,
And still his soul continuously bore
A life in theirs. But less its shine excelled
    Than when I first beheld.

III

His fellow-yearsmen passed, and then
In later hearts I looked for him again;
And found him—shrunk, alas! into a thin
    And spectral mannikin.

IV

Lastly I ask—now old and chill—
If aught of him remain unperished still;
And find, in me alone, a feeble spark,
    Dying amid the dark.

WIVES IN THE SERE

I

Never a careworn wife but shows,
    If a joy suffuse her,
Something beautiful to those
    Patient to peruse her,
Some one charm the world unknows
    Precious to a muser,
Haply what, ere years were foes,
    Moved her mate to choose her.

II

But, be it a hint of rose
    That an instant hues her,
Or some early light or pose
    Wherewith thought renews her—
Seen by him at full, ere woes

Practised to abuse her—
Sparely comes it, swiftly goes,
Time again subdues her.

AN AUGUST MIDNIGHT

I

A shaded lamp and a waving blind,
And the beat of a clock from a distant floor:
On this scene enter—winged, horned, and spined—
A longlegs, a moth, and a dumbledore;
While 'mid my page there idly stands
A sleepy fly, that rubs its hands. . . .

II

Thus meet we five, in this still place,
At this point of time, at this point in space.
—My guests besmear my new-penned line,
Or bang at the lamp and fall supine.
"God's humblest, they!" I muse. Yet why?
They know Earth-secrets that know not I.

MAX GATE.

THE DARKLING THRUSH

I leant upon a coppice gate
    When Frost was spectre-gray,
And Winter's dregs made desolate
    The weakening eye of day.
The tangled bine-stems scored the sky
    Like strings of broken lyres,
And all mankind that haunted nigh
    Had sought their household fires.

The land's sharp features seemed to be
 The Century's corpse outleant,
His crypt the cloudy canopy,
 The wind his death-lament.
The ancient pulse of germ and birth
 Was shrunken hard and dry,
And every spirit upon earth
 Seemed fervourless as I.

At once a voice arose among
 The bleak twigs overhead
In a full-hearted evensong
 Of joy illimited;
An aged thrush, frail, gaunt, and small,
 In blast-beruffled plume,
Had chosen thus to fling his soul
 Upon the growing gloom.

So little cause for carolings
 Of such ecstatic sound
Was written on terrestrial things
 Afar or nigh around,
That I could think there trembled through
 His happy good-night air
Some blessed Hope, whereof he knew
 And I was unaware.

  December 1900.

THE RUINED MAID

"O 'melia, my dear, this does everything crown!
Who could have supposed I should meet you in Town?
And whence such fair garments, such prosperi-ty?"—
"O didn't you know I'd been ruined?" said she.

—"You left us in tatters, without shoes or socks,
Tired of digging potatoes, and spudding up docks;
And now you've gay bracelets and bright feathers three!"—
"Yes: that's how we dress when we're ruined," said she.

—"At home in the barton you said 'thee' and 'thou,'
And 'thik oon,' and 'theäs oon,' and 't'other'; but now
Your talking quite fits 'ee for high compa-ny!"—
"Some polish is gained with one's ruin," said she.

—"Your hands were like paws then, your face blue and bleak
But now I'm bewitched by your delicate cheek,
And your little gloves fit as on any la-dy!"—
"We never do work when we're ruined," said she.

—"You used to call home-life a hag-ridden dream,
And you'd sigh, and you'd sock; but at present you seem
To know not of megrims or melancho-ly!"—
"True. One's pretty lively when ruined," said she.

—"I wish I had feathers, a fine sweeping gown,
And a delicate face, and could strut about Town!"—
"My dear—a raw country girl, such as you be,
Cannot quite expect that. You ain't ruined," said she.

WESTBOURNE PARK VILLAS, 1866.

THE RESPECTABLE BURGHER

ON "THE HIGHER CRITICISM"

Since Reverend Doctors now declare
That clerks and people must prepare
To doubt if Adam ever were;
To hold the flood a local scare;
To argue, though the stolid stare,
That everything had happened ere

27

The prophets to its happening sware;
That David was no giant-slayer,
No one to call a God-obeyer
In certain details we could spare,
But rather was a debonair
Shrewd bandit, skilled as banjo-player:
That Solomon sang the fleshy Fair,
And gave the Church no thought what'er,
That Esther with her royal wear,
And Mordecai, the son of Jair,
And Joshua's triumphs, Job's despair,
And Balaam's ass's bitter blare;
Nebuchadnezzar's furnace-flare,
And Daniel and the den affair,
And other stories rich and rare,
Were writ to make old doctrine wear
Something of a romantic air:
That the Nain widow's only heir,
And Lazarus with cadaverous glare
(As done in oils by Piombo's care)
Did not return from Sheol's lair:
That Jael set a fiendish snare,
That Pontius Pilate acted square.
That never a sword cut Malchus' ear;
And (but for shame I must forbear)
That ____ ____ did not reappear! . . .
—Since thus they hint, nor turn a hair,
All churchgoing will I forswear,
And sit on Sundays in my chair,
And read that moderate man Voltaire.

MEMORY AND I

"O Memory, where is now my youth,
Who used to say that life was truth?"

"I saw him in a crumbled cot
    Beneath a tottering tree;
That he as phantom lingers there
    Is only known to me."

"O Memory, where is now my joy,
Who lived with me in sweet employ?"

"I saw him in gaunt gardens lone,
    Where laughter used to be;
That he as phantom wanders there
    Is known to none but me."

"O Memory, where is now my hope,
Who charged with deeds my skill and scope?"

"I saw her in a tomb of tomes,
    Where dreams are wont to be;
That she as spectre haunteth there
    Is only known to me."

"O Memory, where is now my faith,
One time a champion, now a wraith?"

"I saw her in a ravaged aisle,
    Bowed down on bended knee;
That her poor ghost outflickers there
    Is known to none but me."

"O Memory, where is now my love,
That rayed me as a god above?"

"I saw her in an ageing shape
    Where beauty used to be;
That her fond phantom lingers there
    Is only known to me."

᾽ΑΓΝΩΣΤΩι ΘΕΩι [1]

Long have I framed weak phantasies of Thee,
 O Willer masked and dumb!
 Who makest Life become,—
As though by labouring all-unknowingly,
 Like one whom reveries numb.

How much of consciousness informs Thy will,
 Thy biddings, as if blind,
 Of death-inducing kind,
Nought shows to us ephemeral ones who fill
 But moments in Thy mind.

Perhaps Thy ancient rote-restricted ways
 Thy ripening rule transcends;
 That listless effort tends
To grow percipient with advance of days,
 And with percipience mends.

For, in unwonted purlieus, far and nigh,
 At whiles or short or long,
 May be discerned a wrong
Dying as of self-slaughter; whereat I
 Would raise my voice in song.

AFTER THE CLUB-DANCE

Black'on frowns east on Maidon,
 And westward to the sea,
But on neither is his frown laden
 With scorn, as his frown on me!

---

[1] "To the Unknown God."—Editor.

At dawn my heart grew heavy,
  I could not sip the wine,
I left the jocund bevy
  And that young man o' mine.

The roadside elms pass by me,—
  Why do I sink with shame
When the birds a-perch there eye me?
  They, too, have done the same!

THE HOMECOMING

Gruffly growled the wind on Toller downland broad and bare,
And lonesome was the house, and dark; and few came there.

"Now don't ye rub your eyes so red; we're home and have no cares;
Here's a skimmer-cake for supper, peckled onions, and some pears;
I've got a little keg o' summat strong, too, under stairs:
—What, slight your husband's victuals? Other brides can tackle
  theirs!"

The wind of winter mooed and mouthed their chimney like a horn,
And round the house and past the house 'twas leafless and lorn.

"But my dear and tender poppet, then, how came ye to agree
In Ivel church this morning? Sure, there-right you married me!"
—"Hoo-hoo!—I don't know—I forgot how strange and far 'twould be,
An' I wish I was at home again with dear daddee!"

Gruffly growled the wind on Toller downland broad and bare,
And lonesome was the house, and dark; and few came there.

"I didn't think such furniture as this was all you'd own,
And great black beams for ceiling, and a floor o' wretched stone,
And nasty pewter platters, horrid forks of steel and bone,
And a monstrous crock in chimney. 'Twas to me quite unbeknown!"

Rattle rattle went the door; down flapped a cloud of smoke,
As shifting north the wicked wind assayed a smarter stroke.

"Now sit ye by the fire, poppet; put yourself at ease:
And keep your little thumb out of your mouth, dear, please!
And I'll sing to 'ee a pretty song of lovely flowers and bees,
And happy lovers taking walks within a grove o' trees."

Gruffly growled the wind on Toller Down, so bleak and bare,
And lonesome was the house, and dark; and few came there.

"Now, don't ye gnaw your handkercher; 'twill hurt your little tongue,
And if you do feel spitish, 'tis because ye are over young;
But you'll be getting older, like us all, ere very long,
And you'll see me as I am—a man who never did 'ee wrong."

Straight from Whit'sheet Hill to Benvill Lane the blusters pass,
Hitting hedges, milestones, handposts, trees, and tufts of grass.

"Well, had I only known, my dear, that this was how you'd be,
I'd have married her of riper years that was so fond of me.
But since I can't, I've half a mind to run away to sea,
And leave 'ee to go barefoot to your d—d daddee!"

Up one wall and down the other—past each window-pane—
Prance the gusts, and then away down Crimmercrock's long lane.

"I—I—don't know what to say to't, since your wife I've vowed to be;
And as 'tis done, I s'pose here I must bide—poor me!
Aye—as you are ki-ki-kind, I'll try to live along with 'ee,
Although I'd fain have stayed at home with dear daddee!"

Gruffly growled the wind on Toller Down, so bleak and bare,
And lonesome was the house, and dark; and few came there.

"That's right, my Heart! And though on haunted Toller Down we be,
And the wind swears things in chimley, we'll to supper merrily!

So don't ye tap your shoe so pettish-like; but smile at me,
And ye'll soon forget to sock and sigh for dear daddee!"

THE RASH BRIDE

AN EXPERIENCE OF THE MELLSTOCK QUIRE

I

We Christmas-carolled down the Vale, and up the Vale, and round
    the Vale,
We played and sang that night as we were yearly wont to do—
A carol in a minor key, a carol in the major D,
Then at each house: "Good wishes: many Christmas joys to you!"

II

Next, to the widow's John and I and all the rest drew on. And I
Discerned that John could hardly hold the tongue of him for joy.
The widow was a sweet young thing whom John was bent on
    marrying,
And quiring at her casement seemed romantic to the boy.

III

"She'll make reply, I trust," said he, "to our salute? She must!"
    said he,
"And then I will accost her gently—much to her surprise!—
For knowing not I am with you here, when I speak up and call
    her dear
A tenderness will fill her voice, a bashfulness her eyes."

IV

So, by her window-square we stood; ay, with our lanterns there
    we stood,
And he along with us,—not singing, waiting for a sign;
And when we'd quired her carols three a light was lit and out
    looked she,
A shawl about her bedgown, and her colour red as wine.

V

And sweetly then she bowed her thanks, and smiled, and spoke
 aloud her thanks;
When lo, behind her back there, in the room, a man appeared.
I knew him—one from Woolcomb way—Giles Swetman—honest as
 the day,
But eager, hasty; and I felt that some strange trouble neared.

VI

"How comes he there? . . . Suppose," said we, "she's wed of
 late! Who knows?" said we.
—"She married yester-morning—only mother yet has known
The secret o't!" shrilled one small boy. "But now I've told, let's
 wish 'em joy!"
A heavy fall aroused us: John had gone down like a stone.

VII

We rushed to him and caught him round, and lifted him, and brought
 him round,
When, hearing something wrong had happened, oped the window
 she:
"Has one of you fallen ill?" she asked, "by these night labours over-
 tasked?"
None answered. That she'd done poor John a cruel turn felt we.

VIII

Till up spoke Michael: "Fie, young dame! You've broke your promise,
 sly young dame,
By forming this new tie, young dame, and jilting John so true,
Who trudged to-night to sing to 'ee because he thought he'd bring
 to 'ee
Good wishes as your coming spouse. May ye such trifling rue!"

IX

Her man had said no word at all; but being behind had heard it all,
And now cried: "Neighbours, on my soul I knew not 'twas like this!"
And then to her: "If I had known you'd had in tow not me alone,
No wife should you have been of mine. It is a dear bought bliss!"

34

X

She changed death-white, and heaved a cry: we'd never heard so
  grieved a cry
As came from her at this from him: heartbroken quite seemed she;
And suddenly, as we looked on, she turned, and rushed; and she was
  gone,
Whither, her husband, following after, knew not; nor knew we.

XI

We searched till dawn about the house; within the house, without
  the house,
We searched among the laurel boughs that grew beneath the wall,
And then among the crocks and things, and stores for winter junket-
  ings,
In linhay, loft, and dairy; but we found her not at all.

XII

Then John rushed in: "O friends," he said, "hear this, this, this!" and
  bends his head:
"I've—searched round by the—*well*, and find the cover open wide!
I am fearful that—I can't say what. . . . Bring lanterns, and some
  cords to knot."
We did so, and we went and stood the deep dark hole beside.

XIII

And then they, ropes in hand, and I—ay, John, and all the band, and I
Let down a lantern to the depths—some hundred feet and more;
It glimmered like a fog-dimmed star; and there, beside its light, afar,
White drapery floated, and we knew the meaning that it bore.

XIV

The rest is naught. . . . We buried her o' Sunday. Neighbours car-
  ried her;
And Swetman—he who'd married her—now miserablest of men,
Walked mourning first; and then walked John; just quivering, but
  composed anon;
And we the quire formed round the grave, as was the custom then.

XV

Our old bass player, as I recall—his white hair blown—but why
    recall!—
His viol unstrapped, bent figure—doomed to follow her full soon—
Stood bowing, pale and tremulous; and next to him the rest of
    us. . . .
We sang the Ninetieth Psalm to her—set to Saint Stephen's tune.

NIGHT IN THE OLD HOME

When the wasting embers redden the chimney-breast,
And Life's bare pathway looms like a desert track to me,
And from hall and parlour the living have gone to their rest,
My perished people who housed them here come back to me.

They come and seat them around in their mouldy places,
Now and then bending towards me a glance of wistfulness,
A strange upbraiding smile upon all their faces,
And in the bearing of each a passive tristfulness.

"Do you uphold me, lingering and languishing here,
A pale late plant of your once strong stock?" I say to them;
"A thinker of crooked thoughts upon Life in the sere,
And on That which consigns men to night after showing the day to
    them?"

"—O let be the Wherefore! We fevered our years not thus:
Take of Life what it grants, without question!" they answer me
    seemingly.
"Enjoy, suffer, wait: spread the table here freely like us,
And, satisfied, placid, unfretting, watch Time away beamingly!"

NEW YEAR'S EVE*

"I have finished another year," said God,
      "In grey, green, white, and brown;
I have strewn the leaf upon the sod,
Sealed up the worm within the clod,
      And let the last sun down."

"And what's the good of it?" I said
      "What reasons made you call
From formless void this earth we tread,
When nine-and-ninety can be read
      Why nought should be at all?

"Yea, Sire; why shaped you us, 'who in
      This tabernacle groan'—
If ever a joy be found herein,
Such joy no man had wished to win
      If he had never known!"

GOD'S EDUCATION

I saw him steal the light away
      That haunted in her eye:
It went so gently none could say
More than that it was there one day
      And missing by-and-by.

I watched her longer, and he stole
      Her lily tincts and rose;
All her young sprightliness of soul
Next fell beneath his cold control,
      And disappeared like those.

I asked: "Why do you serve her so?
      Do you, for some glad day,

* The last three stanzas of this poem, which were omitted from the
first printing, appear on page 132.

Hoard these her sweets—?" He said, "O no,
They charm not me; I bid Time throw
　　Them carelessly away."

Said I: "We call that cruelty—
　　We, your poor mortal kind."
He mused. "The thought is new to me.
Forsooth, though I men's master be,
　　Theirs is the teaching mind!"

THE MAN HE KILLED

　　"Had he and I but met
　　By some old ancient inn,
We should have sat us down to wet
　　Right many a nipperkin!

　　"But ranged as infantry,
　　And staring face to face,
I shot at him as he at me,
　　And killed him in his place.

　　"I shot him dead because—
　　Because he was my foe,
Just so: my foe of course he was;
　　That's clear enough; although

　　"He thought he'd 'list, perhaps,
　　Off-hand like—just as I—
Was out of work—had sold his traps—
　　No other reason why.

　　"Yes; quaint and curious war is!
　　You shoot a fellow down
You'd treat if met where any bar is,
　　Or help to half-a-crown."

　　1902.

WAGTAIL AND BABY

A baby watched a ford, whereto
    A wagtail came for drinking;
A blaring bull went wading through,
    The wagtail showed no shrinking.

A stallion splashed his way across,
    The birdie nearly sinking;
He gave his plumes a twitch and toss,
    And held his own unblinking.

Next saw the baby round the spot
    A mongrel slowly slinking;
The wagtail gazed, but faltered not
    In dip and sip and prinking.

A perfect gentleman then neared;
    The wagtail, in a winking,
With terror rose and disappeared;
    The baby fell a-thinking.

CHANNEL FIRING

That night your great guns, unawares,
Shook all our coffins as we lay,
And broke the chancel window-squares,
We thought it was the Judgment-day

And sat upright. While drearisome
Arose the howl of wakened hounds:
The mouse let fall the altar-crumb,
The worms drew back into the mounds,

The glebe cow drooled. Till God called, "No;
It's gunnery practice out at sea

Just as before you went below;
The world is as it used to be:

"All nations striving strong to make
Red war yet redder. Mad as hatters
They do no more for Christés sake
Than you who are helpless in such matters.

"That this is not the judgment-hour
For some of them's a blessed thing,
For if it were they'd have to scour
Hell's floor for so much threatening. . . .

"Ha, ha. It will be warmer when
I blow the trumpet (if indeed
I ever do; for you are men,
And rest eternal sorely need)."

So down we lay again. "I wonder,
Will the world ever saner be,"
Said one, "than when He sent us under
In our indifferent century!"

And many a skeleton shook his head.
"Instead of preaching forty year,"
My neighbour Parson Thirdly said,
"I wish I had stuck to pipes and beer."

Again the guns disturbed the hour,
Roaring their readiness to avenge,
As far inland as Stourton Tower,
And Camelot, and starlit Stonehenge.

April 1914.

> night time tranquility

"WHEN I SET OUT FOR LYONNESSE" [1]

(1870)

When I set out for Lyonnesse,
　　A hundred miles away,
　　The rime was on the spray,
And starlight lit my lonesomeness
When I set out for Lyonnesse
　　A hundred miles away.

What would bechance at Lyonnesse
　　While I should sojourn there
　　No prophet durst declare,
Nor did the wisest wizard guess
What would bechance at Lyonnesse
　　While I should sojourn there.

When I came back from Lyonnesse
　　With magic in my eyes,
　　All marked with mute surmise
My radiance rare and fathomless,
When I came back from Lyonnesse
　　With magic in my eyes!

THE CONVERGENCE OF THE TWAIN

(LINES ON THE LOSS OF THE "TITANIC")

I

In a solitude of the sea
　　Deep from human vanity,
And the Pride of Life that planned her, stilly couches she.

---

[1] Hardy was going to St. Juliot, in Cornwall, near the scene of fabled Lyonnesse, to design the rebuilding of a church; he was to meet there Emma Lavinia Gifford, whom he would marry.—Editor.

II

Steel chambers, late the pyres
Of her salamandrine fires,
Cold currents thrid, and turn to rhythmic tidal lyres.

III

Over the mirrors meant
To glass the opulent
The sea-worm crawls—grotesque, slimed, dumb, indifferent.

IV

Jewels in joy designed
To ravish the sensuous mind
Lie lightless, all their sparkles bleared and black and blind.

V

Dim moon-eyed fishes near
Gaze at the gilded gear
And query: "What does this vaingloriousness down here?" . . .

VI

Well: while was fashioning
This creature of cleaving wing,
The Immanent Will that stirs and urges everything

cleaving together sense as in Biblical sense of marriage

hull of ship

VII

Prepared a sinister mate
For her—so gaily great—
A Shape of Ice, for the time far and dissociate.

VIII

And as the smart ship grew
In stature, grace, and hue,
In shadowy silent distance grew the Iceberg too.

IX

Alien they seemed to be:
No mortal eye could see
The intimate welding of their later history,

(wedding)

X

Or sign that they were bent
By paths coincident
On being anon twin halves of one august event,

XI

Till the Spinner of the Years
Said "Now!" And each one hears,
And consummation comes, and jars two hemispheres.

WESSEX HEIGHTS

(1896)

There are some heights in Wessex, shaped as if by a kindly hand
For thinking, dreaming, dying on, and at crises when I stand,
Say, on Ingpen Beacon eastward, or on Wylls-Neck westwardly,
I seem where I was before my birth, and after death may be.

In the lowlands I have no comrade, not even the lone man's friend—
Her who suffereth long and is kind; accepts what he is too weak to
     mend:
Down there they are dubious and askance; there nobody thinks as I,
But mind-chains do not clank where one's next neighbour is the sky.

In the towns I am tracked by phantoms having weird detective
     ways—
Shadows of beings who fellowed with myself of earlier days:
They hang about at places, and they say harsh heavy things—
Men with a wintry sneer, and women with tart disparagings.

Down there I seem to be false to myself, my simple self that was,
And is not now, and I see him watching, wondering what crass cause
Can have merged him into such a strange continuator as this,
Who yet has something in common with himself, my chrysalis.

I cannot go to the great grey Plain; there's a figure against the moon,
Nobody sees it but I, and it makes my breast beat out of tune;

I cannot go to the tall-spired town, being barred by the forms now
    passed
For everybody but me, in whose long vision they stand there fast.

There's a ghost at Yell'ham Bottom chiding loud at the fall of the
    night,
There's a ghost in Froom-side Vale, thin lipped and vague, in a
    shroud of white,
There is one in the railway train whenever I do not want it near,
I see its profile against the pane, saying what I would not hear.

As for one rare fair woman, I am now but a thought of hers,
I enter her mind and another thought succeeds me that she prefers;
Yet my love for her in its fullness she herself even did not know;
Well, time cures hearts of tenderness, and now I can let her go.

So I am found on Ingpen Beacon, or on Wylls-Neck to the west,
Or else on homely Bulbarrow, or little Pilsdon Crest,
Where men have never cared to haunt, nor women have walked with
    me,
And ghosts then keep their distance; and I know some liberty.

"AH, ARE YOU DIGGING ON MY GRAVE?"

"Ah, are you digging on my grave
        My loved one?—planting rue?"
—"No: yesterday he went to wed
One of the brightest wealth has bred.
'It cannot hurt her now,' he said,
        'That I should not be true.'"

"Then who is digging on my grave?
        My nearest dearest kin?"
—"Ah, no: they sit and think, 'What use!
What good will planting flowers produce?

No tendance of her mound can loose
    Her spirit from Death's gin.'"

"But some one digs upon my grave?
    My enemy?—prodding sly?"
—"Nay: when she heard you had passed the Gate
That shuts on all flesh soon or late,
She thought you no more worth her hate,
    And cares not where you lie."

"Then, who is digging on my grave?
    Say—since I have not guessed!"
—"O it is I, my mistress dear,
Your little dog, who still lives near,
And much I hope my movements here
    Have not disturbed your rest?"

"Ah, yes! *You* dig upon my grave . . .
    Why flashed it not on me
That one true heart was left behind!
What feeling do we ever find
To equal among human kind
    A dog's fidelity!"

"Mistress, I dug upon your grave
    To bury a bone, in case
I should be hungry near this spot
When passing on my daily trot.
I am sorry, but I quite forgot
    It was your resting-place."

THE GOING

Why did you give no hint that night
That quickly after the morrow's dawn,
And calmly, as if indifferent quite,

You would close your term here, up and be gone
　　　Where I could not follow
　　　With wing of swallow
To gain one glimpse of you ever anon!

　　　Never to bid good-bye,
　　　Or lip me the softest call,
Or utter a wish for a word, while I
Saw morning harden upon the wall,
　　　Unmoved, unknowing
　　　That your great going
Had place that moment, and altered all.

Why do you make me leave the house
And think for a breath it is you I see
At the end of the alley of bending boughs
Where so often at dusk you used to be;
　　　Till in darkening dankness
　　　The yawning blankness
Of the perspective sickens me!

　　　You were she who abode
　　　By those red-veined rocks far West,
You were the swan-necked one who rode
Along the beetling Beeny Crest,
　　　And, reining nigh me,
　　　Would muse and eye me,
While Life unrolled us its very best.

Why, then, latterly did we not speak,
Did we not think of those days long dead,
And ere your vanishing strive to seek
That time's renewal? We might have said,
　　　"In this bright spring weather
　　　We'll visit together
Those places that once we visited."

Well, well! All's past amend,
    Unchangeable. It must go.
I seem but a dead man held on end
To sink down soon. . . . O you could not know
        That such swift fleeing
        No soul foreseeing—
Not even I—would undo me so!

December 1912.

RAIN ON A GRAVE

Clouds spout upon her
    Their waters amain
    In ruthless disdain,—
Her who but lately
    Had shivered with pain
As at touch of dishonour
If there had lit on her
So coldly, so straightly
    Such arrows of rain:

One who to shelter
    Her delicate head
Would quicken and quicken
    Each tentative tread
If drops chanced to pelt her
    That summertime spills
    In dust-paven rills
When thunder-clouds thicken
    And birds close their bills.

Would that I lay there
    And she were housed here!
Or better, together
Were folded away there
Exposed to one weather

We both,—who would stray there
When sunny the day there,
  Or evening was clear
  At the prime of the year.

Soon will be growing
  Green blades from her mound,
And daisies be showing
  Like stars on the ground,
Till she form part of them—
Ay—the sweet heart of them,
Loved beyond measure
With a child's pleasure
  All her life's round.

January 31, 1913.

"I FOUND HER OUT THERE"

I found her out there
On a slope few see,
That falls westwardly
To the salt-edged air,
Where the ocean breaks
On the purple strand,
And the hurricane shakes
The solid land.

I brought her here,
And have laid her to rest
In a noiseless nest
No sea beats near.
She will never be stirred
In her loamy cell
By the waves long heard
And loved so well.

So she does not sleep
By those haunted heights
The Atlantic smites
And the blind gales sweep,
Whence she often would gaze
At Dundagel's famed head,
While the dipping blaze
Dyed her face fire-red;

And would sigh at the tale
Of sunk Lyonnesse,
As a wind-tugged tress
Flapped her cheek like a flail;
Or listen at whiles
With a thought-bound brow
To the murmuring miles
She is far from now.

Yet her shade, maybe,
Will creep underground
Till it catch the sound
Of that western sea
As it swells and sobs
Where she once domiciled,
And joy in its throbs
With the heart of a child.

BEENY CLIFF

(MARCH 1870–MARCH 1913)

Poe-like

I

O the opal and the sapphire of that wandering western sea,
And the woman riding high above with bright hair flapping free—
The woman whom I loved so, and who loyally loved me.

II

The pale mews plained below us, and the waves seemed far away
In a nether sky, engrossed in saying their ceaseless babbling say,
As we laughed light-heartedly aloft on that clear-sunned March day.

III

A little cloud then cloaked us, and there flew an irised rain,
And the Atlantic dyed its levels with a dull misfeatured stain,
And then the sun burst out again, and purples prinked the main.

IV

—Still in all its chasmal beauty bulks old Beeny to the sky,
And shall she and I not go there once again now March is nigh,
And the sweet things said in that March say anew there by and by?

V

What if still in chasmal beauty looms that wild weird western shore,
The woman now is—elsewhere—whom the ambling pony bore,
And nor knows nor cares for Beeny, and will laugh there nevermore.

AQUAE SULIS

The chimes called midnight, just at interlune,
And the daytime parle on the Roman investigations
Was shut to silence, save for the husky tune
The bubbling waters played near the excavations.

And a warm air came up from underground,
And a flutter, as of a filmy shape unsepulchred,
That collected itself, and waited, and looked around:
Nothing was seen, but utterances could be heard:

Those of the Goddess whose shrine was beneath the pile
Of the God with the baldachined altar overhead:
"And what did you win by raising this nave and aisle
Close on the site of the temple I tenanted?

"The notes of your organ have thrilled down out of view
To the earth-clogged wrecks of my edifice many a year,
Though stately and shining once—ay, long ere you
Had set up crucifix and candle here.

"Your priests have trampled the dust of mine without rueing,
Despising the joys of man whom I so much loved,
Though my springs boil on by your Gothic arcades and pewing,
And sculptures crude. . . . Would Jove they could be removed!"

"Repress, O lady proud, your traditional ires;
You know not by what a frail thread we equally hang;
It is said we are images both—twitched by people's desires;
And that I, as you, fail like a song men yesterday sang!"

"What—a Jumping-jack you, and myself but a poor Jumping-jill,
Now worm-eaten, times agone twitched at Humanity's bid?
O I cannot endure it!—But, chance to us whatso there will,
Let us kiss and be friends! Come, agree you?"—None heard if he
    did. . . .

And the olden dark hid the cavities late laid bare,
And all was suspended and soundless as before,
Except for a gossamery noise fading off in the air,
And the boiling voice of the waters' medicinal pour.

BATH.

HAD YOU WEPT

Had you wept; had you but neared me with a hazed uncertain ray,
Dewy as the face of the dawn, in your large and luminous eye,
Then would have come back all the joys the tidings had slain that
    day,
And a new beginning, a fresh fair heaven, have smoothed the things
    awry.
But you were less feebly human, and no passionate need for clinging

51

Possessed your soul to overthrow reserve when I came near;
Ay, though you suffer as much as I from storms the hours are bring-
     ing
Upon your heart and mine, I never see you shed a tear.

The deep strong woman is weakest, the weak one is the strong;
The weapon of all weapons best for winning, you have not used;
Have you never been able, or would you not, through the evil times
     and long?
Has not the gift been given you, or such gift have you refused?
When I bade me not absolve you on that evening or the morrow,
Why did you not make war on me with those who weep like rain?
You felt too much, so gained no balm for all your torrid sorrow,
And hence our deep division, and our dark undying pain.

STARLINGS ON THE ROOF

"No smoke spreads out of this chimney-pot,
The people who lived here have left the spot,
And others are coming who knew them not.

"If you listen anon, with an ear intent,
The voices, you'll find, will be different
From the well-known ones of those who went."

"Why did they go? Their tones so bland
Were quite familiar to our band;
The comers we shall not understand."

"They look for a new life, rich and strange;
They do not know that, let them range
Wherever they may, they will get no change.

"They will drag their house-gear ever so far
In their search for a home no miseries mar;
They will find that as they were they are,

"That every hearth has a ghost, alack,
And can be but the scene of a bivouac
Till they move their last—no care to pack!"

THE MOON LOOKS IN

I

I have risen again,
And awhile survey
By my chilly ray
Through your window-pane
Your upturned face,
As you think, "Ah—she
Now dreams of me
In her distant place!"

II

I pierce her blind
In her far-off home:
She fixes a comb,
And says in her mind,
"I start in an hour;
Whom shall I meet?
Won't the men be sweet,
And the women sour!"

AT TEA [1]

The kettle descants in a cosy drone,
And the young wife looks in her husband's face,
And then at her guest's, and shows in her own
Her sense that she fills an envied place;

[1] This and the seven following poems are from *Satires of Circumstance.*—
Editor.

And the visiting lady is all abloom,
And says there was never so sweet a room.

And the happy young housewife does not know
That the woman beside her was first his choice,
Till the fates ordained it could not be so. . . .
Betraying nothing in look or voice
The guest sits smiling and sips her tea,
And he throws her a stray glance yearningly.

IN CHURCH

"And now to God the Father," he ends,
And his voice thrills up to the topmost tiles:
Each listener chokes as he bows and bends,
And emotion pervades the crowded aisles.
Then the preacher glides to the vestry-door,
And shuts it, and thinks he is seen no more.

The door swings softly ajar meanwhile,
And a pupil of his in the Bible class,
Who adores him as one without gloss or guile,
Sees her idol stand with a satisfied smile
And re-enact at the vestry-glass
Each pulpit gesture in deft dumb-show
That had moved the congregation so.

BY HER AUNT'S GRAVE

"Sixpence a week," says the girl to her lover,
"Aunt used to bring me, for she could confide
In me alone, she vowed. 'Twas to cover
The cost of her headstone when she died.
And that was a year ago last June;
I've not yet fixed it. But I must soon."

"And where is the money now, my dear?"
"O, snug in my purse. . . . Aunt was *so* slow
In saving it—eighty weeks, or near." . . .
"Let's spend it," he hints. "For she won't know.
There's a dance to-night at the Load of Hay."
She passively nods. And they go that way.

IN THE ROOM OF THE BRIDE-ELECT

"Would it had been the man of our wish!"
Sighs her mother. To whom with vehemence she
In the wedding-dress—the wife to be—
"Then why were you so mollyish
As not to insist on him for me!"
The mother, amazed: "Why, dearest one,
Because you pleaded for this or none!"

"But Father and you should have stood out strong!
Since then, to my cost, I have lived to find
That you were right and that I was wrong;
This man is a dolt to the one declined. . . .
Ah!—here he comes with his button-hole rose.
Good God—I must marry him I suppose!"

IN THE CEMETERY

"You see those mothers squabbling there?"
Remarks the man of the cemetery.
"One says in tears, ' *'Tis mine lies here!*'
Another, *'Nay, mine, you Pharisee!'*
Another, *'How dare you move my flowers
And put your own on this grave of ours!'*
But all their children were laid therein
At different times, like sprats in a tin."

"And then the main drain had to cross,
And we moved the lot some nights ago,
And packed them away in the general foss
With hundreds more. But their folks don't know,
And as well cry over a new-laid drain
As anything else, to ease your pain!"

OUTSIDE THE WINDOW

"My stick!" he says, and turns in the lane
To the house just left, whence a vixen voice
Comes out with the firelight through the pane,
And he sees within that the girl of his choice
Stands rating her mother with eyes aglare
For something said while he was there.

"At last I behold her soul undraped!"
Thinks the man who had loved her more than himself;
"My God!—'tis but narrowly I have escaped.—
My precious porcelain proves it delf."
His face has reddened like one ashamed,
And he steals off, leaving his stick unclaimed.

OVER THE COFFIN

They stand confronting, the coffin between,
His wife of old, and his wife of late,
And the dead man whose they both had been
Seems listening aloof, as to things past date.
—"I have called," says the first. "Do you marvel or not?"
"In truth," says the second, "I do—somewhat."

"Well, there was a word to be said by me! . . .
I divorced that man because of you—

It seemed I must do it, boundenly;
But now I am older, and tell you true,
For life is little, and dead lies he;
I would I had let alone you two!
And both of us, scorning parochial ways,
Had lived like the wives in the patriarchs' days."

IN THE MOONLIGHT

"O lonely workman, standing there
In a dream, why do you stare and stare
At her grave, as no other grave there were?

"If your great gaunt eyes so importune
Her soul by the shine of this corpse-cold moon,
Maybe you'll raise her phantom soon!"

"Why, fool, it is what I would rather see
Than all the living folk there be;
But alas, there is no such joy for me!"

"Ah—she was one you loved, no doubt,
Through good and evil, through rain and drought
And when she passed, all your sun went out?"

"Nay: she was the woman I did not love,
Whom all the others were ranked above,
Whom during her life I thought nothing of."

TO THE MOON

"What have you looked at, Moon,
    In your time,
Now long past your prime?"

"O, I have looked at, often looked at
        Sweet, sublime,
Sore things, shudderful, night and noon
        In my time."

"What have you mused on, Moon,
        In your day,
So aloof, so far away?"
"O, I have mused on, often mused on
        Growth, decay
Nations alive, dead, mad, aswoon,
        In my day!"

"Have you much wondered, Moon,
        On your rounds,
Self-wrapt, beyond Earth's bounds?"
"Yea, I have wondered, often wondered
        At the sounds
Reaching me of the human tune
        On my rounds."

"What do you think of it, Moon,
        As you go?
Is Life much, or no?"
"O, I think of it, often think of it
        As a show
God ought surely to shut up soon,
        As I go."

THE BLINDED BIRD

So zestfully canst thou sing?
And all this indignity,
With God's consent, on thee!
Blinded ere yet a-wing
By the red-hot needle thou,

I stand and wonder how
So zestfully thou canst sing!

Resenting not such wrong,
Thy grievous pain forgot,
Eternal dark thy lot,
Groping thy whole life long,
After that stab of fire;
Enjailed in pitiless wire;
Resenting not such wrong!

Who hath charity? This bird.
Who suffereth long and is kind,
Is not provoked, though blind
And alive ensepulchred?
Who hopeth, endureth all things?
Who thinketh no evil, but sings?
Who is divine? This bird.

"THE WIND BLEW WORDS"

The wind blew words along the skies,
    And these it blew to me
Through the wide dusk: "Lift up your eyes,
    Behold this troubled tree,
Complaining as it sways and plies;
    It is a limb of thee.

"Yea, too, the creatures sheltering round—
    Dumb figures, wild and tame,
Yea, too, thy fellows who abound—
    Either of speech the same
Or far and strange—black, dwarfed, and browned,
    They are stuff of thy own frame."

I moved on in a surging awe
    Of inarticulateness

At the pathetic Me I saw
  In all his huge distress,
Making self-slaughter of the law
  To kill, break, or suppress.

THE OXEN

Christmas Eve, and twelve of the clock.
  "Now they are all on their knees,"
An elder said as we sat in a flock
  By the embers in hearthside ease.

We pictured the meek mild creatures where
  They dwelt in their strawy pen,
Nor did it occur to one of us there
  To doubt they were kneeling then.

So fair a fancy few would weave
  In these years! Yet, I feel,
If someone said on Christmas Eve,
  "Come; see the oxen kneel,

"In the lonely barton by yonder coomb
  Our childhood used to know,"
I should go with him in the gloom,
  Hoping it might be so.

TRANSFORMATIONS

Portion of this yew
Is a man my grandsire knew,
Bosomed here at its foot:
This branch may be his wife,

A ruddy human life
Now turned to a green shoot.

These grasses must be made
Of her who often prayed,
Last century, for repose;
And the fair girl long ago
Whom I often tried to know
May be entering this rose.

So, they are not underground,
But as nerves and veins abound
In the growths of upper air,
And they feel the sun and rain,
And the energy again
That made them what they were!

GREAT THINGS

Sweet cyder is a great thing,
   A great thing to me,
Spinning down to Weymouth town
   By Ridgway thirstily,
And maid and mistress summoning
   Who tend the hostelry:
O cyder is a great thing,
   A great thing to me!

The dance it is a great thing,
   A great thing to me,
With candles lit and partners fit
   For night-long revelry;
And going home when day-dawning
   Peeps pale upon the lea:
O dancing is a great thing,
   A great thing to me!

Love is, yea, a great thing,
  A great thing to me,
When, having drawn across the lawn
  In darkness silently,
A figure flits like one a-wing
  Out from the nearest tree:
O love is, yes, a great thing,
  A great thing to me!

Will these be always great things,
  Great things to me? . . .
Let it befall that One will call,
  "Soul, I have need of thee":
What then? Joy-jaunts, impassioned flings,
  Love, and its ecstasy,
Will always have been great things,
  Great things to me!

THE BLOW [1]

That no man schemed it is my hope—
Yea, that it fell by will and scope
    Of That Which some enthrone,
And for whose meaning myriads grope.

For I would not that of my kind
There should, of his unbiassed mind,
    Have been one known
Who such a stroke could have designed;

Since it would augur works and ways
Below the lowest that man assays
    To have hurled that stone
Into the sunshine of our days!

[1] The blow is the World War.—Editor.

And if it prove that no man did,
And that the Inscrutable, the Hid,
    Was cause alone
Of this foul crash our lives amid,

I'll go in due time, and forget
In some deep graveyard's oubliette
    The thing whereof I groan,
And cease from troubling; thankful yet

Time's finger should have stretched to show
No aimful author's was the blow
    That swept us prone,
But the Immanent Doer's That doth not know

Which in some age unguessed of us
May lift Its blinding incubus,
    And see, and own:
"It grieves me I did thus and thus!"

LOVE THE MONOPOLIST

(YOUNG LOVER'S REVERIE)

The train draws forth from the station-yard,
    And with it carries me.
I rise, and stretch out, and regard
    The platform left, and see
An airy slim blue form there standing,
    And know that it is she.

While with strained vision I watch on,
    The figure turns round quite
To greet friends gaily; then is gone. . . .
    The import may be slight,
But why remained she not hard gazing
    Till I was out of sight?

"O do not chat with others there,"
　　I brood. "They are not I.
O strain your thoughts as if they were
　　Gold bands between us; eye
All neighbour scenes as so much blankness
　　Till I again am by!

"A troubled soughing in the breeze
　　And the sky overhead
Let yourself feel; and shadeful trees,
　　Ripe corn, and apples red,
Read as things barren and distasteful
　　While we are separated!

"When I come back uncloak your gloom.
　　And let in lovely day;
Then the long dark as of the tomb
　　Can well be thrust away
With sweet things I shall have to practise,
　　And you will have to say!"

Begun 1871 : *finished*——

THE INTERLOPER

"And I saw the figure and visage of Madness seeking for a home."

There are three folk driving in a quaint old chaise,
And the cliff-side track looks green and fair:
I view them talking in quiet glee
As they drop down towards the puffins' lair
　　By the roughest of ways;
But another with the three rides on, I see,
　　Whom I like not to be there!

No: it's not anybody you think of. Next
A dwelling appears by a slow sweet stream

Where two sit happy and half in the dark:
They read, helped out by a frail-wick'd gleam,
    Some rhythmic text;
But one sits with them whom they don't mark,
    One I'm wishing could not be there.

No: not whom you knew and name. And now
I discern gay diners in a mansion-place,
And the guests dropping wit—pert, prim, or choice,
And the hostess's tender and laughing face,
    And the host's bland brow;
But I cannot help hearing a hollow voice,
    And I'd fain not hear it there.

No: it's not from the stranger you met once. Ah,
Yet a goodlier scene than that succeeds;
People on a lawn—quite a crowd of them. Yes,
And they chatter and ramble as fancy leads;
    And they say, "Hurrah!"
To a blithe speech made; save one, mirthless,
    Who ought not to be there.

Nay: it's not the pale Form your imagings arise,
That waits on us all at a destined time,
It is not the Fourth Figure the Furnace showed;
O that it were such a shape sublime
    In these latter days!
It is that under which best lives corrode;
    Would, would it could not be there!

THE FIVE STUDENTS

The sparrow dips in his wheel-rut bath,
    The sun grows passionate-eyed,
And boils the dew to smoke by the paddock-path;
    As strenuously we stride,—

Five of us; dark He, fair He, dark She, fair She, I,
　　All beating by.

The air is shaken, the high-road hot,
　　Shadowless swoons the day,
The greens are sobered and cattle at rest; but not
　　We on our urgent way,—
Four of us; fair She, dark She, fair He, I, are there,
　　But one—elsewhere.

Autumn moulds the hard fruit mellow,
　　And forward still we press
Through moors, briar-meshed plantations, clay-pits yellow,
　　As in the spring hours—yes,
Three of us; fair He, fair She, I, as heretofore,
　　But—fallen one more.

The leaf drops: earthworms draw it in
　　At night-time noiselessly,
The fingers of birch and beech are skeleton-thin,
　　And yet on the beat are we,—
Two of us; fair she, I. But no more left to go
　　The track we know.

Icicles tag the church-aisle leads,
　　The flag-rope gibbers hoarse,
The home-bound foot-folk wrap their snow-flaked heads,
　　Yet I still stalk the course—
One of us. . . . Dark and fair He, dark and fair She, gone
　　The rest—anon.

THE WIND'S PROPHECY

I travel on by barren farms,
And gulls glint out like silver flecks
Against a cloud that speaks of wrecks,

And bellies down with black alarms.
I say: "Thus from my lady's arms
I go; those arms I love the best!"
The wind replies from dip and rise,
"Nay; toward her arms thou journeyest."

A distant verge morosely gray
Appears, while clots of flying foam
Break from its muddy monochrome,
And a light blinks up far away.
I sigh: "My eyes now as all day
Behold her ebon loops of hair!"
Like bursting bonds the wind responds,
"Nay, wait for tresses flashing fair!"

From tides the lofty coastlands screen
Come smitings like the slam of doors,
Or hammerings on hollow floors,
As the swell cleaves through caves unseen.
Say I: "Though broad this wild terrene,
Her city home is matched of none!"
From the hoarse skies the wind replies:
"Thou shouldst have said her sea-bord one."

The all-prevailing clouds exclude
The one quick timorous transient star;
The waves outside where breakers are
Huzza like a mad multitude.
"Where the sun ups it, mist-imbued,"
I cry, "there reigns the star for me!"
The wind outshrieks from points and peaks:
"Here, westward, where it downs, mean ye!"

Yonder the headland, vulturine,
Snores like old Skrymer in his sleep,
And every chasm and every steep
Blackens as wakes each pharos-shine
"I roam, but one is safely mine,"

I say. "God grant she stay my own!"
Low laughs the wind as if it grinned:
"Thy Love is one thou'st not yet known."

DURING WIND AND RAIN

They sing their dearest songs—
He, she, all of them—yea,
Treble and tenor and bass,
    And one to play;
With the candles mooning each face. . . .
    Ah, no; the years O!
How the sick leaves reel down in throngs!

They clear the creeping moss—
Elders and juniors—aye,
Making the pathway neat
    And the garden gay;
And they build a shady seat. . . .
    Ah, no; the years, the years;
See, the white storm-birds wing across!

They are blithely breakfasting all—
Men and maidens—yea,
Under the summer tree,
    With a glimpse of the bay,
While pet fowl come to the knee. . . .
    Ah, no; the years O!
And the rotten rose is ript from the wall.

They change to a high new house,
He, she, all of them—aye,
Clocks and carpets, and chairs
    On the lawn all day,
And brightest things that are theirs. . . .
    Ah, no; the years, the years;
Down their carved names the rain-drop ploughs.

"Why do you weep there, O sweet lady,
Why do you weep before that brass?—
(I'm a mere student sketching the mediaeval)
Is some late death lined there, alas?—
Your father's? . . . Well, all pay the debt that paid he!"

"Young man, O must I tell!—My husband's! And under
His name I set mine, and my *death!*—
Its date left vacant till my heirs should fill it,
Stating me faithful till my last breath."
—"Madam, that you are a widow wakes my wonder!"

"O wait! For last month I—remarried!
And now I fear 'twas a deed amiss.
We've just come home. And I am sick and saddened
At what the new one will say to this;
And will he think—think that I should have tarried?

"I may add, surely,—with no wish to harm him—
That he's a temper—yes, I fear!
And when he comes to church next Sunday morning,
And sees that written. . . . O dear, O dear!"
—"Madam, I swear your beauty will disarm him!"

JUBILATE

"The very last time I ever was here," he said.
"I saw much less of the quick than I saw of the dead."
—He was a man I had met with somewhere before,
But how or when I now could recall no more.

"The hazy mazy moonlight at one in the morning
Spread out as a sea across the frozen snow,
Glazed to live sparkles like the great breastplate adorning
The priest of the Temple, with Urim and Thummim aglow.

69

"The yew-tree arms, glued hard to the stiff stark air,
Hung still in the village sky as theatre-scenes
When I came by the churchyard wall, and halted there
At a shut-in sound of fiddles and tambourines.

"And as I stood hearkening, dulcimers, hautboys, and shawms,
And violoncellos, and a three-stringed double-bass,
Joined in, and were intermixed with a singing of psalms;
And I looked over at the dead men's dwelling-place.

"Through the shine of the slippery snow I now could see,
As it were through a crystal roof, a great company
Of the dead minueting in stately step underground
To the tune of the instruments I had before heard sound.

"It was 'Eden New,' and dancing they sang in a chore,
'We are out of it all!—yea, in Little-Ease cramped no more!'
And their shrouded figures pacing with joy I could see
As you see the stage from the gallery. And they had no heed of me.

"And I lifted my head quite dazed from the churchyard wall
And I doubted not that it warned I should soon have my call.
But—" . . . Then in the ashes he emptied the dregs of his cup,
And onward he went, and the darkness swallowed him up.

PATHS OF FORMER TIME

No; no;
It must not be so:
They are the ways we do not go.

Still chew
The kine, and moo
In the meadows we used to wander through;

Still purl
The rivulets and curl
Towards the weirs with a musical swirl;

Haymakers
As in former years
Rake rolls into heaps that the pitchfork rears;

Wheels crack
On the turfy track
The wagon pursues with its toppling pack.

"Why then shun—
Since summer's not done—
All this because of the lack of one?"

Had you been
Sharer of that scene
You would not ask while it bites in keen

Why it is so
We can no more go
By the summer paths we used to know!

1913.

THE SHADOW ON THE STONE

I went by the Druid stone
That broods in the garden white and lone,
And I stopped and looked at the shifting shadows
That at some moments fall thereon
From the tree hard by with a rhythmic swing,
And they shaped in my imagining
To the shade that a well-known head and shoulders
Threw there when she was gardening.

I thought her behind my back,
Yea, her I long had learned to lack,
And I said: "I am sure you are standing behind me,
    Though how do you get into this old track?"
    And there was no sound but the fall of a leaf
    As a sad response; and to keep down my grief
I would not turn my head to discover
    That there was nothing in my belief.

    Yet I wanted to look and see
    That nobody stood at the back of me;
But I thought once more: "Nay, I'll not unvision
    A shape which, somehow, there may be."
    So I went on softly from the glade,
    And left her behind me throwing her shade,
As she were indeed an apparition—
    My head unturned lest my dream should fade.

Begun 1913 : *finished* 1916.

IN THE GARDEN

(M. H.)

We waited for the sun
To break its cloudy prison
(For day was not yet done,
And night still unbegun)
Leaning by the dial.

After many a trial—
We all silent there—
It burst as new-arisen,
Throwing a shade to where
Time travelled at that minute.

Little saw we in it,
But this much I know,
Of lookers on that shade,
Her towards whom it made
Soonest had to go.[1]

WHILE DRAWING IN A CHURCHYARD

"It is sad that so many of worth,
  Still in the flesh," soughed the yew,
"Misjudge their lot whom kindly earth
    Secludes from view.

"They ride their diurnal round
  Each day-span's sum of hours
In peerless ease, without jolt or bound
    Or ache like ours.

"If the living could but hear
  What is heard by my roots as they creep
Round the restful flock, and the things said there
    No one would weep."

" 'Now set among the wise,'
  They say: 'Enlarged in scope,
That no God trumpet us to rise
    We truly hope.' "

I listened to his strange tale
  In the mood that stillness brings,
And I grew to accept as the day wore pale
    That show of things.

[1] The person whose life passed at the moment of shadow was Mary, the poet's sister.—Editor.

"FOR LIFE I HAD NEVER CARED GREATLY"

For Life I had never cared greatly,
      As worth a man's while;
      Peradventures unsought,
      Peradventures that finished in nought,
Had kept me from youth and through manhood till lately
      Unwon by its style.

In earliest years—why I know not—
      I viewed it askance;
      Conditions of doubt,
      Conditions that leaked slowly out,
May haply have bent me to stand and to show not
      Much zest for its dance.

With symphonies soft and sweet colour
      It courted me then,
      Till evasions seemed wrong,
      Till evasions gave in to its song,
And I warmed, until living aloofly loomed duller
      Than life among men.

Anew I found nought to set eyes on,
      When, lifting its hand,
      It uncloaked a star,
      Uncloaked it from fog-damps afar,
And showed its beams burning from pole to horizon
      As bright as a brand.

And so, the rough highway forgetting,
      I pace hill and dale
      Regarding the sky,
      Regarding the vision on high,
And thus re-illumed have no humour for letting
      My pilgrimage fail.

IN TIME OF "THE BREAKING OF NATIONS"[1]

I

Only a man harrowing clods
   In a slow silent walk
With an old horse that stumbles and nods
   Half asleep as they stalk.

II

Only thin smoke without flame
   From the heaps of couch-grass;
Yet this will go onward the same
   Though Dynasties pass.

III

Yonder a maid and her wight
   Come whispering by:
War's annals will fade into night
   Ere their story die.

A NEW YEAR'S EVE IN WAR TIME

I

Phantasmal fears,
   And the flap of the flame,
   And the throb of the clock,
   And a loosened slate,
   And the blind night's drone,
Which tiredly the spectral pines intone!

II

And the blood in my ears
   Strumming always the same.
   And the gable-cock

[1] Jer. li, 20.

With its fitful grate,
And myself, alone.

III

The twelfth hour nears
Hand-hid, as in shame;
I undo the lock,
And listen, and wait
For the Young Unknown.

IV

In the dark there careers—
As if Death astride came
To numb all with his knock—
A horse at mad rate
Over rut and stone.

V

No figure appears,
No call of my name,
No sound but "Tic-toc"
Without check. Past the gate
It clatters—is gone.

VI

What rider it bears
There is none to proclaim;
And the Old Year has struck,
And, scarce animate.
The New makes moan.

VII

Maybe that "More Tears!—
More Famine and Flame—
More Severance and Shock!"
Is the order from Fate
That the Rider speeds on
To pale Europe; and tiredly the pines intone.

1915–1916.

"I LOOKED UP FROM MY WRITING"

I looked up from my writing,
   And gave a start to see,
As if rapt in my inditing,
   The moon's full gaze on me.

Her meditative misty head
   Was spectral in its air,
And I involuntarily said,
   "What are you doing there?"

"Oh, I've been scanning pond and hole
   And waterway hereabout
For the body of one with a sunken soul
   Who has put his life-light out.

"Did you hear his frenzied tattle?
   It was sorrow for his son
Who is slain in brutish battle,
   Though he has injured none.

"And now I am curious to look
   Into the blinkered mind
Of one who wants to write a book
   In a world of such a kind."

Her temper overwrought me,
   And I edged to shun her view,
For I felt assured she thought me
   One who should drown him too.

AFTERWARDS

When the Present has latched its postern behind my tremulous stay,
   And the May month flaps its glad green leaves like wings,
Delicate-filmed as new-spun silk, will the neighbours say,
   "He was a man who used to notice such things"?

If it be in the dusk when, like an eyelid's soundless blink,
  The dewfall-hawk comes crossing the shades to alight
Upon the wind-warped upland thorn, a gazer may think,
  "To him this must have been a familiar sight."

If I pass during some nocturnal blackness, mothy and warm,
  When the hedgehog travels furtively over the lawn,
One may say, "He strove that such innocent creatures should come
    to no harm,
  But he could do little for them; and now he is gone."

If, when hearing that I have been stilled at last, they stand at the
    door,
  Watching the full-starred heavens that winter sees,
Will this thought rise on those who will meet my face no more,
  "He was one who had an eye for such mysteries"?

And will any say when my bell of quittance is heard in the gloom,
  And a crossing breeze cuts a pause in its outrollings,
Till they rise again, as they were a new bell's boom,
  "He hears it not now, but used to notice such things"?

WEATHERS

I

  This is the weather the cuckoo likes,
    And so do I;
  When showers betumble the chestnut spikes,
    And nestlings fly:
  And the little brown nightingale bills his best,
  And they sit outside at "The Travellers' Rest,"
  And maids come forth sprig-muslin drest,
  And citizens dream of the south and west,
    And so do I.

This is the weather the shepherd shuns,
    And so do I;
When beeches drip in browns and duns,
    And thresh, and ply;
And hill-hid tides throb, throe on throe,
And meadow rivulets overflow,
And drops on gate-bars hang in a row,
And rooks in families homeward go,
    And so do I.

THE GARDEN SEAT

Its former green is blue and thin,
And its once firm legs sink in and in;
Soon it will break down unaware,
Soon it will break down unaware.

At night when reddest flowers are black
Those who once sat thereon come back;
Quite a row of them sitting there,
Quite a row of them sitting there.

With them the seat does not break down,
Nor winter freeze them, nor floods drown,
For they are as light as upper air,
They are as light as upper air!

"ACCORDING TO THE MIGHTY WORKING"

I

When moiling seems at cease
    In the vague void of night-time,
    And heaven's wide roomage stormless

Between the dusk and light-time,
And fear at last is formless,
We call the allurement Peace.

II

Peace, this hid riot, Change,
This revel of quick-cued mumming,
This never truly being,
This evermore becoming,
This spinner's wheel onfleeing
Outside perception's range.

GOING AND STAYING

I

The moving sun-shapes on the spray,
The sparkles where the brook was flowing,
Pink faces, plightings, moonlit May,
These were the things we wished would stay;
But they were going.

II

Seasons of blankness as of snow,
The silent bleed of a world decaying,
The moan of multitudes in woe,
These were the things we wished would go;
But they were staying.

III

Then we looked closelier at Time,
And saw his ghostly arms revolving
To sweep off woeful things with prime,
Things sinister with things sublime
Alike dissolving.

HER SONG

I sang that song on Sunday,
    To witch an idle while,
I sang that song on Monday,
    As fittest to beguile;
I sang it as the year outwore,
    And the new slid in;
I thought not what might shape before
    Another would begin.

I sang that song in summer,
    All unforeknowingly,
To him as a new-comer
    From regions strange to me:
I sang it when in afteryears
    The shades stretched out,
And paths were faint; and flocking fears
    Brought cup-eyed care and doubt.

Sings he that song on Sundays
    In some dim land afar,
On Saturdays, or Mondays,
    As when the evening star
Glimpsed in upon his bending face,
    And my hanging hair,
And time untouched me with a trace
    Of soul-smart or despair?

"AND THERE WAS A GREAT CALM"

(ON THE SIGNING OF THE ARMISTICE, NOV. 11, 1918)

I

There had been years of Passion—scorching, cold,
And much Despair, and Anger heaving high,
Care whitely watching, Sorrows manifold,

81

Among the young, among the weak and old,
And the pensive Spirit of Pity whispered, "Why?"

II

Men had not paused to answer. Foes distraught
Pierced the thinned peoples in a brute-like blindness,
Philosophies that sages long had taught,
And Selflessness, were as an unknown thought,
And "Hell!" and "Shell!" were yapped at Lovingkindness.

III

The feeble folk at home had grown full-used
To "dug-outs," "snipers," "Huns," from the war-adept
In the mornings heard, and at evetides perused;
To day-dreamt men in millions, when they mused—
To nightmare-men in millions when they slept.

IV

Waking to wish existence timeless, null,
Sirius they watched above where armies fell;
He seemed to check his flapping when, in the lull
Of night a boom came thencewise, like the dull
Plunge of a stone dropped into some deep well.

V

So, when old hopes that earth was bettering slowly
Were dead and damned, there sounded "War is done!"
One morrow. Said the bereft, and meek, and lowly,
"Will men some day be given to grace? yea, wholly,
And in good sooth, as our dreams used to run?"

VI

Breathless they paused. Out there men raised their glance
To where had stood those poplars lank and lopped,
As they had raised it through the four years' dance
Of Death in the now familiar flats of France;
And murmured, "Strange, this! How? All firing stopped?"

VII

Aye; all was hushed. The about-to-fire fired not,
The aimed-at moved away in trance-lipped song.
One checkless regiment slung a clinching shot
And turned. The Spirit of Irony smirked out, "What?
Spoil peradventures woven of Rage and Wrong?"

VIII

Thenceforth no flying fires inflamed the gray,
No hurtlings shook the dewdrop from the thorn,
No moan perplexed the mute bird on the spray;
Worn horses mused: "We are not whipped to-day";
No weft-winged engines blurred the moon's thin horn.

IX

Calm fell. From Heaven distilled a clemency;
There was peace on earth, and silence in the sky;
Some could, some could not, shake off misery:
The Sinister Spirit sneered: "It had to be!"
And again the Spirit of Pity whispered, "Why?"

HAUNTING FINGERS

A PHANTASY IN A MUSEUM OF MUSICAL INSTRUMENTS

"Are you awake,
    Comrades, this silent night?
Well 'twere if all of our glossy gluey make
Lay in the damp without, and fell to fragments quite!"

"O viol, my friend,
    I watch, though Phosphor nears,
And I fain would drowse away to its utter end
This dumb dark stowage after our loud melodious years!"

And they felt past handlers clutch them,
    Though none was in the room,

83

Old players' dead fingers touch them,
        Shrunk in the tomb.

" 'Cello, good mate,
    You speak my mind as yours:
Doomed to this voiceless, crippled, corpselike state,
Who, dear to famed Amphion, trapped here, long endures?"

    "Once I could thrill
    The populace through and through,
Wake them to passioned pulsings past their will." . . .
(A contra-basso spake so, and the rest sighed anew.)

And they felt old muscles travel
        Over their tense contours,
And with long skill unravel
        Cunningest scores.

    "The tender pat
    Of her aery finger-tips
Upon me daily—I rejoiced thereat!"
(Thuswise a harpsicord, as 'twere from dampered lips.)

    "My keys' white shine,
    Now sallow, met a hand
Even whiter. . . . Tones of hers fell forth with mine
In sowings of sound so sweet no lover could withstand!"

And its clavier was filmed with fingers
        Like tapering flames—wan, cold—
Or the nebulous light that lingers
        In charnel mould.

    "Gayer than most
    Was I," reverbed a drum;
"The regiments, marchings, throngs, hurrahs! What a host
I stirred—even when crape mufflings gagged me well-nigh dumb!"

Trilled an aged viol:
"Much tune have I set free
To spur the dance, since my first timid trial
Where I had birth—far hence, in sun-swept Italy!"

And he feels apt touches on him
From those that pressed him then;
Who seem with their glance to con him,
Saying, "Not again!"

"A holy calm,"
Mourned a shawm's voice subdued,
"Steeped my Cecilian rhythms when hymn and psalm
Poured from devout souls met in Sabbath sanctitude."

"I faced the sock
Nightly," twanged a sick lyre,
"Over ranked lights! O charm of life in mock,
O scenes that fed love, hope, wit, rapture, mirth, desire!"

Thus they, till each past player
Stroked thinner and more thin,
And the morning sky grew grayer
And day crawled in.

THE TWO HOUSES

In the heart of night,
When farers were not near,
The left house said to the house on the right,
"I have marked your rise, O smart newcomer here."

Said the right, cold-eyed:
"Newcomer here I am,
Hence haler than you with your cracked old hide,
Loose casements, wormy beams, and doors that jam.

"Modern my wood,
    My hangings fair of hue;
  While my windows open as they should,
And water-pipes thread all my chambers through.

    "Your gear is gray,
    Your face wears furrows untold."
  "—Yours might," mourned the other, "if you held, brother
The Presences from aforetime that I hold.

    "You have not known
    Men's lives, deaths, toils, and teens;
  You are but a heap of stick and stone;
A new house has no sense of the have-beens.

    "Void as a drum
    You stand: I am packed with these,
  Though, strangely, living dwellers who come
See not the phantoms all my substance sees!

    "Visible in the morning
    Stand they, when dawn drags in;
  Visible at night; yet hint or warning
Of these thin elbowers few of the inmates win.

    "Babes new brought-forth
    Obsess my rooms; straight-stretched
  Lank corpses, ere outborne to earth;
Yea, throng they as when first from the Byss unfetched.

    "Dancers and singers
    Throb in me now as once;
  Rich-noted throats and gossamered flingers
Of heels; the learned in love-lore and the dunce.

    "Note here within
    The bridegroom and the bride,

Who smile and greet their friends and kin,
And down my stairs depart for tracks untried.

"Where such inbe,
A dwelling's character
Takes theirs, and a vague semblancy
To them in all its limbs, and light, and atmosphere.

"Yet the blind folk
My tenants, who come and go
In the flesh mid these, with souls unwoke,
Of such sylph-like surrounders do not know."

"—Will the day come,"
Said the new one, awestruck, faint,
"When I shall lodge shades dim and dumb—
And with such spectral guests become acquaint?"

"—That will it, boy;
Such shades will people thee,
Each in his misery, irk, or joy,
And print on thee their presences as on me."

"I WORKED NO WILE TO MEET YOU"

(SONG)

I worked no wile to meet you,
    My sight was set elsewhere,
I sheered about to shun you,
    And lent your life no care.
I was unprimed to greet you
    At such a date and place,
Constraint alone had won you
    Vision of my strange face!

You did not seek to see me
    Then or at all, you said,
—Meant passing when you neared me
    But stumbling-blocks forbade.
You even had thought to flee me,
    By other mindings moved;
No influent star endeared me,
    Unknown, unrecked, unproved!

What, then, was there to tell us
    The flux of flustering hours
Of their own tide would bring us
    By no device of ours
To where the daysprings well us
    Heart-hydromels that cheer,
Till Time enearth and swing us
    Round with the turning sphere.

SIDE BY SIDE

So there sat they,
The estranged two,
Thrust in one pew
By chance that day;
Placed so, breath-nigh,
Each comer unwitting
Who was to be sitting
In touch close by.

Thus side by side
Blindly alighted,
They seemed united
As groom and bride,
Who'd not communed
For many years—
Lives from twain spheres
With hearts distuned.

Her fringes brushed
His garment's hem
As the harmonies rushed
Through each of them:
Her lips could be heard
In the creed and psalms,
And their fingers neared
At the giving of alms.

And women and men,
The matins ended,
By looks commended
Them, joined again.
Quickly said she,
"Don't undeceive them—
Better thus leave them":
"Quite so," said he.

Slight words!—the last
Between them said,
Those two, once wed,
Who had not stood fast.
Diverse their ways
From the western door,
To meet no more
In their span of days.

ON THE TUNE CALLED THE
OLD-HUNDRED-AND-FOURTH

We never sang together
  Ravenscroft's terse old tune
On Sundays or on weekdays,
In sharp or summer weather,
  At night-time or at noon.

Why did we never sing it,
    Why never so incline
On Sundays or on weekdays? . . .
Even when soft wafts would wing it
    From your far floor to mine?

Shall we that tune, then, never
    Stand voicing side by side
On Sundays or on weekdays? . . .
Or shall we, when for ever
    In Sheol we abide,

Sing it in desolation,
    As we might long have done
On Sundays or on weekdays
With love and exultation
    Before our sands had run?

VOICES FROM THINGS GROWING
IN A CHURCHYARD

These flowers are I, poor Fanny Hurd,
            Sir or Madam,
A little girl here sepultured.
Once I flit-fluttered like a bird
Above the grass, as now I wave
In daisy shapes above my grave,
            All day cheerily,
            All night eerily!

—I am one Bachelor Bowring, "Gent,"
            Sir or Madam;
In shingled oak my bones were pent;
Hence more than a hundred years I spent
In my feat of change from a coffin-thrall
To a dancer in green as leaves on a wall,

All day cheerily,
All night eerily!

—I, these berries of juice and gloss,
        Sir or Madam,
Am clean forgotten as Thomas Voss;
Thin-urned, I have burrowed away from the moss
That covers my sod, and have entered this yew,
And turned to clusters ruddy of view,
        All day cheerily,
        All night eerily!

—The Lady Gertrude, proud, high-bred,
        Sir or Madam,
Am I—this laurel that shades your head;
Into its veins I have stilly sped,
And made them of me; and my leaves now shine,
As did my satins superfine,
        All day cheerily,
        All night eerily!

—I, who as innocent withwind climb,
        Sir or Madam,
Am one Eve Greensleeves, in olden time
Kissed by men from many a clime,
Beneath sun, stars, in blaze, in breeze,
As now by glowworms and by bees,
        All day cheerily,
        All night eerily! [1]

—I'm old Squire Audeley Grey, who grew,
        Sir or Madam,
Aweary of life, and in scorn withdrew;
Till anon I clambered up anew
As ivy-green, when my ache was stayed,
And in that attire I have longtime gayed

---

[1] It was said her real name was Eve Trevillian or Trevelyan; and that she was the handsome mother of two or three illegitimate children, *circa* 1784–1795.

All day cheerily,
All night eerily!

—And so these maskers breathe to each
                    Sir or Madam
Who lingers there, and their lively speech
Affords an interpreter much to teach,
As their murmurous accents seem to come
Thence hitheraround in a radiant hum,
                    All day cheerily,
                    All night eerily!

BY HENSTRIDGE CROSS AT THE YEAR'S END

(From this centuries-old cross-road the highway leads
east to London, north to Bristol and Bath, west to Exeter
and the Land's End, and south to the Channel coast.)

Why go the east road now? . . .
That way a youth went on a morrow
After mirth, and he brought back sorrow
        Painted upon his brow:
        Why go the east road now?

Why go the north road now?
Torn, leaf-strewn, as if scoured by foemen,
Once edging fiefs of my forefolk yeomen,
        Fallows fat to the plough:
        Why go the north road now?

Why go the west road now?
Thence to us came she, bosom-burning,
Welcome with joyousness returning. . . .
        She sleeps under the bough:
        Why go the west road now?

Why go the south road now?
That way marched they some are forgetting,
Stark to the moon left, past regretting
    Loves who have falsed their vow. . . .
    Why go the south road now?

Why go any road now?
White stands the handpost for brisk onbearers,
"Halt!" is the word for wan-cheeked farers
    Musing on Whither, and How. . . .
    Why go any road now?

"Yea: we want new feet now"
Answer the stones. "Want chit-chat, laughter:
Plenty of such to go hereafter
    By our tracks, we trow!
    We are for new feet now."

During the War.

AFTER THE WAR

Last Post sounded
Across the mead
To where he loitered
With absent heed.
Five years before
In the evening there
Had flown that call
To him and his Dear.
"You'll never come back;
Good-bye!" she had said;
"Here I'll be living,
And my Love dead!"

Those closing minims
Had been as shafts darting

93

Through him and her pressed
In that last parting;
They thrilled him not now,
In the selfsame place
With the selfsame sun
On his war-seamed face.
"Lurks a god's laughter
In this?" he said,
"That I am the living
And she the dead!"

THE CHAPEL-ORGANIST

(A.D. 185–)

I've been thinking it through, as I play here to-night, to play never
    again,
By the light of that lowering sun peering in at the window-pane,
And over the back-street roofs, throwing shades from the boys of the
    chore
In the gallery, right upon me, sitting up to these keys once more. . . .
How I used to hear tongues ask, as I sat here when I was new.
"Who is she playing the organ? She touches it mightily true!"
"She travels from Havenpool Town," the deacon would softly speak,
"The stipend can hardly cover her fare hither twice in the week."
(It fell far short of doing, indeed; but I never told,
For I have craved minstrelsy more than lovers, or beauty, or gold.)

'Twas so he answered at first, but the story grew different later:
"It cannot go on much longer, from what we hear of her now!"
At the meaning wheeze in the words the inquirer would shift his
    place
Till he could see round the curtain that screened me from people
    below.
"A handsome girl," he would murmur, upstaring (and so I am).
"But—too much sex in her build; fine eyes, but eyelids too heavy;

A bosom too full for her age; in her lips too voluptuous a dye."
(It may be. But who put it there? Assuredly it was not I.)

I went on playing and singing when this I had heard, and more,
Though tears half-blinded me; yes, I remained going on and on,
Just as I used me to chord and to sing at the selfsame time! . . .
For it's a contralto—my voice is; they'll hear it again here to-night
In the psalmody notes that I love far beyond every lower delight.

Well, the deacon, in fact, that day had learnt new tidings about me;
They troubled his mind not a little, for he was a worthy man.
(He trades as a chemist in High Street, and during the week he had
     sought
His fellow-deacon, who throve as a bookbinder over the way.)
"These are strange rumours," he said. "We must guard the good
     name of the chapel.
If, sooth, she's of evil report, what else can we do but dismiss her?"
"—But get such another to play here we cannot for double the price!"
It settled the point for the time, and I triumphed awhile in their
     strait,
And my much-beloved grand semibreves went living on, pending
     my fate.

At length in the congregation more headshakes and murmurs were
     rife,
And my dismissal was ruled, though I was not warned of it then.
But a day came when they declared it. The news entered me as a
     sword;
I was broken; so pallid of face that they thought I should faint, they
     said.
I rallied. "O, rather than go, I will play you for nothing!" said I.
'Twas in much desperation I spoke it, for bring me to forfeit I could
     not
Those melodies chorded so richly for which I had laboured and
     lived.
They paused. And for nothing I played at the chapel through Sun-
     days again,

Upheld by that art which I loved more than blandishments lavished of men.

But it fell that murmurs anew from the flock broke the pastor's peace.
Some member had seen me at Havenpool, comrading close a sea-captain.
(O yes; I was thereto constrained, lacking means for the fare to and fro.)
Yet God knows, if aught He knows ever, I loved the Old-Hundredth, Saint Stephen's,
Mount Zion, New Sabbath, Miles-Lane, Holy Rest, and Arabia, and Eaton,
Above all embraces of body by wooers who sought me and won! . . .
Next week 'twas declared I was seen coming home with a swain ere the sun.

The deacons insisted then, strong; and forgiveness I did not implore.
I saw all was lost for me, quite, but I made a last bid in my throbs.
My bent, finding victual in lust, men's senses had libelled my soul,
But the soul should die game, if I knew it! I turned to my masters and said:
"I yield, Gentlemen, without parlance. But—let me just hymn you *once* more!
It's a little thing, Sirs, that I ask; and a passion is music with me!"
They saw that consent would cost nothing, and show as good grace, as knew I,
Though tremble I did, and feel sick, as I paused thereat, dumb for their words.
They gloomily nodded assent, saying, "Yes, if you care to. Once more,
And only once more, understand." To that with a bend I agreed.
—"You've a fixed and a far-reaching look," spoke one who had eyed me awhile.
"I've a fixed and a far-reaching plan, and my look only showed it," I smile.

This evening of Sunday is come—the last of my functioning here.
"She plays as if she were possessed!" they exclaim, glancing upward
and round.
"Such harmonies I never dreamt the old instrument capable of!"
Meantime the sun lowers and goes; shades deepen; the lights are
turned up,
And the people voice out the last singing: tune Tallis: the Evening
Hymn.
(I wonder Dissenters sing Ken: it shows them more liberal in spirit
At this little chapel down here than at certain new others I know.)
I sing as I play. Murmurs some one: "No woman's throat richer than
hers!"
"True: in these parts," think I. "But, my man, never more will its
richness outspread."
And I sing with them onward: "The grave dread as little do I as my
bed."

I lift up my feet from the pedals; and then, while my eyes are still
wet
From the symphonies born of my fingers, I do that whereon I am set,
And draw from my "full round bosom" (their words; how can *I* help
its heave?)
A bottle blue-coloured and fluted—a vinaigrette, they may conceive—
And before the choir measures my meaning, reads aught in my
moves to and fro,
I drink from the phial at a draught, and they think it a pick-me-up;
so.
Then I gather my books as to leave, bend over the keys as to pray.
When they come to me motionless, stooping, quick death will have
whisked me away.

"Sure, nobody meant her to poison herself in her haste, after all!"
The deacons will say as they carry me down and the night shadows
fall,
"Though the charges were true," they will add. "It's a case red as
scarlet withal!"
I have never once minced it. Lived chaste I have not. Heaven knows
it above! . . .

But past all the heavings of passion—it's music has been my life-
    love! . . .
That tune did go well—this last playing! . . . I reckon they'll bury
    me here. . . .
Not a soul from the seaport my birthplace—will come, or bestow
    me . . . a tear.

AT THE ENTERING OF THE NEW YEAR

I

(OLD STYLE)

Our songs went up and out the chimney,
And roused the home-gone husbandmen;
Our allemands, our heys, poussettings,
Our hands-across and back again,
Sent rhythmic throbbings through the casements
    On to the white highway,
Where nighted farers paused and muttered,
    "Keep it up well, do they!"

The contrabasso's measured booming
Sped at each bar to the parish bounds,
To shepherds at their midnight lambings,
To stealthy poachers on their rounds;
And everybody caught full duly
    The notes of our delight,
As Time unrobed the Youth of Promise
    Hailed by our sanguine sight.

II

(NEW STYLE)

We stand in the dusk of a pine-tree limb,
As if to give ear to the muffled peal,
Brought or withheld at the breeze's whim;

But our truest heed is to words that steal
From the mantled ghost that looms in the gray,
And seems, so far as our sense can see,
To feature bereaved Humanity,
As it sighs to the imminent year its say:—

"O stay without, O stay without,
Calm comely Youth, untasked, untired;
Though stars irradiate thee about
Thy entrance here is undesired.
Open the gate not, mystic one;
Must we avow what we would close confine?
With thee, good friend, we would have converse none,
Albeit the fault may not be thine."

December 31. During the War.

A PROCESSION OF DEAD DAYS

I see the ghost of a perished day;
I know his face, and the feel of his dawn:
'Twas he who took me far away
    To a spot strange and gray:
Look at me, Day, and then pass on,
But come again: yes, come anon!

Enters another into view;
His features are not cold or white,
But rosy as a vein seen through:
    Too soon he smiles adieu.
Adieu, O ghost-day of delight;
But come and grace my dying sight.

Enters the day that brought the kiss:
He brought it in his foggy hand
To where the mumbling river is,
    And the high clematis;

It lent new colour to the land,
And all the boy within me manned.

Ah, this one. Yes, I know his name,
He is the day that wrought a shine
Even on a precinct common and tame,
    As 'twere of purposed aim.
He shows him as a rainbow sign
Of promise made to me and mine.

The next stands forth in his morning clothes,
And yet, despite their misty blue,
They mark no sombre custom-growths
    That joyous living loathes,
But a meteor act, that left in its queue
A train of sparks my lifetime through.

I almost tremble at his nod—
This next in train—who looks at me
As I were slave, and he were god
    Wielding an iron rod.
I close my eyes; yet still is he
In front there, looking mastery.

In semblance of a face averse
The phantom of the next one comes:
I did not know what better or worse
    Chancings might bless or curse
When his original glossed the thrums
Of ivy, bringing that which numbs.

Yes; trees were turning in their sleep
Upon their windy pillows of gray
When he stole in. Silent his creep
    On the grassed eastern steep. . . .
I shall not soon forget that day,
And what his third hour took away!

HE FOLLOWS HIMSELF

In a heavy time I dogged myself
    Along a louring way,
Till my leading self to my following self
    Said: "Why do you hang on me
      So harassingly?"

"I have watched you, Heart of mine," I cried,
    "So often going astray
And leaving me, that I have pursued,
    Feeling such truancy
      Ought not to be."

He said no more, and I dogged him on
    From noon to the dun of day
By prowling paths, until anew
    He begged: "Please turn and flee!—
      What do you see?"

"Methinks I see a man," said I,
    "Dimming his hours to gray.
I will not leave him while I know
    Part of myself is he
      Who dreams such dree!"

"I go to my old friend's house," he urged,
    "So do not watch me, pray!"
"Well, I will leave you in peace," said I,
    "Though of this poignancy
      You should fight free:

"Your friend, O other me, is dead;
    You know not what you say."
—"That do I! And at his green-grassed door
    By night's bright galaxy
      I bend a knee."

—The yew-plumes moved like mockers' beards
  Though only boughs were they,
And I seemed to go; yet still was there,
  And am, and there haunt we
    Thus bootlessly.

THE SINGING WOMAN

There was a singing woman
  Came riding across the mead
At the time of the mild May weather,
  Tameless, tireless;
This song she sung: "I am fair, I am young!"
  And many turned to heed.

And the same singing woman
  Sat crooning in her need
At the time of the winter weather;
  Friendless, fireless,
She sang this song: "Life, thou'rt too long!"
  And there was none to heed.

VAGG HOLLOW

(Vagg Hollow is a marshy spot on the old Roman
Road near Ilchester, where "things" are seen. Mer-
chandise was formerly fetched inland from the canal-
boats at Load-Bridge by waggons this way.)

"What do you see in Vagg Hollow,
Little boy, when you go
In the morning at five on your lonely drive?"
"—I see men's souls, who follow
Till we've passed where the road lies low,
When they vanish at our creaking!

"They are like white faces speaking
Beside and behind the waggon—
One just as father's was when here.
The waggoner drinks from his flagon,
(Or he'd flinch when the Hollow is near)
But he does not give me any.

"Sometimes the faces are many;
But I walk along by the horses,
He asleep on the straw as we jog;
And I hear the loud water-courses,
And the drops from the trees in the fog,
And watch till the day is breaking,

"And the wind out by Tintinhull waking;
I hear in it father's call
As he called when I saw him dying,
And he sat by the fire last Fall,
And mother stood by sighing;
But I'm not afraid at all!"

THE COUNTRY WEDDING

(A FIDDLER'S STORY)

Little fogs were gathered in every hollow,
But the purple hillocks enjoyed fine weather
As we marched with our fiddles over the heather
—How it comes back!—to their wedding that day.

Our getting there brought our neighbours and all, O!
Till, two and two, the couples stood ready.
And her father said: "Souls, for God's sake, be steady!"
And we strung up our fiddles, and sounded out "A."

The groomsman he stared, and said, "You must follow!"
But we'd gone to fiddle in front of the party,

(Our feelings as friends being true and hearty)
And fiddle in front we did—all the way.

Yes, from their door by Mill-tail-Shallow,
And up Styles-Lane, and by Front-Street houses,
Where stood maids, bachelors, and spouses,
Who cheered the songs that we knew how to play.

I bowed the treble before her father,
Michael the tenor in front of the lady,
The bass-viol Reub—and right well played he!—
The serpent Jim; ay, to church and back.

I thought the bridegroom was flurried rather,
As we kept up the tune outside the chancel,
While they were swearing things none can cancel
Inside the walls to our drumstick's whack.

"Too gay!" she pleaded. "Clouds may gather,
And sorrow come." But she gave in, laughing,
And by supper-time when we'd got to the quaffing
Her fears were forgot, and her smiles weren't slack.

A grand wedding 'twas! And what would follow
We never thought. Or that we should have buried her
On the same day with the man that married her,
A day like the first, half hazy, half clear.

Yes: little fogs were in every hollow,
Though the purple hillocks enjoyed fine weather,
When we went to play 'em to church together,
And carried 'em there in an after year.

THE MASTER AND THE LEAVES

I

We are budding, Master, budding,
  We of your favourite tree;
March drought and April flooding
  Arouse us merrily,
Our stemlets newly studding;
  And yet you do not see!

II

We are fully woven for summer
  In stuff of limpest green,
The twitterer and the hummer
  Here rest of nights, unseen,
While like a long-roll drummer
  The nightjar thrills the treen.

III

We are turning yellow, Master,
  And next we are turning red,
And faster then and faster
  Shall seek our rooty bed,
All wasted in disaster!
  But you lift not your head.

IV

—"I mark your early going,
  And that you'll soon be clay,
I have seen your summer showing
  As in my youthful day;
But why I seem unknowing
  Is too sunk in to say!"

ON ONE WHO LIVED AND DIED
WHERE HE WAS BORN

When a night in November
  Blew forth its bleared airs
An infant descended
  His birth-chamber stairs
  For the very first time,
  At the still, midnight chime;
All unapprehended
  His mission, his aim.—
Thus, first, one November,
An infant descended
    The stairs.

On a night in November
  Of weariful cares,
A frail aged figure
  Ascended those stairs
  For the very last time:
  All gone his life's prime,
All vanished his vigour,
  And fine, forceful frame:
Thus, last, one November
Ascended that figure
    Upstairs.

On those nights in November—
  Apart eighty years—
The babe and the bent one
  Who traversed those stairs
  From the early first time
  To the last feeble climb—
That fresh and that spent one—
  Were even the same:
Yea, who passed in November
As infant, as bent one,
    Those stairs.

Wise child of November!
　　From birth to blanched hairs
Descending, ascending,
　　Wealth-wantless, those stairs;
　　Who saw quick in time
　　As a vain pantomime
Life's tending, its ending,
　　The worth of its fame.
Wise child of November,
Descending, ascending
　　Those stairs!

"I WAS THE MIDMOST"

I was the midmost of my world
　　When first I frisked me free,
For though within its circuit gleamed
　　But a small company,
And I was immature, they seemed
　　To bend their looks on me.

She was the midmost of my world
　　When I went further forth,
And hence it was that, whether I turned
　　To south, east, west, or north,
Beams of an all-day Polestar burned
　　From that new axe of earth.

Where now is midmost in my world?
　　I trace it not at all:
No midmost shows it here, or there,
　　When wistful voices call
"We are fain! We are fain!" from everywhere
　　On Earth's bewildering ball!

THE WHIPPER-IN

"My father was the whipper-in,—
    Is still—if I'm not misled?
And now I see, where the hedge is thin,
    A little spot of red;
    Surely it is my father
    Going to the kennel-shed!

"I cursed and fought my father—aye,
    And sailed to a foreign land;
And feeling sorry, I'm back, to stay,
    Please God, as his helping hand.
    Surely it is my father
    Near where the kennels stand?"

"—True. Whipper-in he used to be
    For twenty years or more;
And you did go away to sea
    As youths have done before.
    Yes, oddly enough that red there
    Is the very coat he wore.

"But he—he's dead; was thrown somehow,
    And gave his back a crick,
And though that is his coat, 'tis now
    The scarecrow of a rick;
    You'll see when you get nearer—
    'Tis spread out on a stick.

"You see, when all had settled down
    Your mother's things were sold,
And she went back to her own town,
    And the coat, ate out with mould,
    Is now used by the farmer
    For scaring, as 'tis old."

THE MILESTONE
BY THE RABBIT-BURROW

(ON YELL'HAM HILL)

In my loamy nook
As I dig my hole
I observe men look
At a stone, and sigh
As they pass it by
To some far goal.

Something it says
To their glancing eyes
That must distress
The frail and lame,
And the strong of frame
Gladden or surprise.

Do signs on its face
Declare how far
Feet have to trace
Before they gain
Some blest champaign
Where no gins are?

THE SEVEN TIMES

The dark was thick. A boy he seemed at that time
   Who trotted by me with uncertain air;
"I'll tell my tale," he murmured, "for I fancy
   A friend goes there? . . ."

Then thus he told. "I reached—'twas for the first time—
   A dwelling. Life was clogged in me with care;
I thought not I should meet an eyesome maiden,
   But found one there.

"I entered on the precincts for the second time—
    'Twas an adventure fit and fresh and fair—
I slackened in my footsteps at the porchway,
        And found her there.

"I rose and travelled thither for the third time,
    The hope-hues growing gayer and yet gayer
As I hastened round the boscage of the outskirts,
        And found her there.

"I journeyed to the place again the fourth time
    (The best and rarest visit of the rare,
As it seemed to me, engrossed about these goings),
        And found her there.

"When I bent me to my pilgrimage the fifth time
    (Soft-thinking as I journeyed I would dare
A certain word at token of good auspice),
        I found her there.

"That landscape did I traverse for the sixth time,
    And dreamed on what we purposed to prepare;
I reached a tryst before my journey's end came,
        And found her there.

"I went again—long after—aye, the seventh time;
    The look of things was sinister and bare
As I caught no customed signal, heard no voice call,
        Nor found her there.

"And now I gad the globe—day, night, and any time,
    To light upon her hiding unaware,
And, maybe, I shall nigh me to some nymph-niche,
        And find her there!"

"But how," said I, "has your so little lifetime
    Given roomage for such loving, loss, despair?
A boy so young!" Forthwith I turned my lantern
        Upon him there.

His head was white. His small form, fine aforetime,
  Was shrunken with old age and battering wear,
An eighty-years long plodder saw I pacing
    Beside me there.

DRAWING DETAILS IN AN OLD CHURCH

I hear the bell-rope sawing,
And the oil-less axle grind,
As I sit alone here drawing
What some Gothic brain designed;
And I catch the toll that follows
    From the lagging bell,
Ere it spreads to hills and hollows
    Where people dwell.

I ask not whom it tolls for,
Incurious who he be;
So, some morrow, when those knolls for
One unguessed, sound out for me,
A stranger, loitering under
    In nave or choir,
May think, too, "Whose, I wonder?"
    But not inquire.

AN ANCIENT TO ANCIENTS

Where once we danced, where once we sang,
        Gentlemen,
The floors are sunken, cobwebs hang,
And cracks creep; worms have fed upon
The doors. Yea, sprightlier times were then
Than now, with harps and tabrets gone,
        Gentlemen!

111

Where once we rowed, where once we sailed,
    Gentlemen,
And damsels took the tiller, veiled
Against too strong a stare (God wot
Their fancy, then or anywhen!)
Upon that shore we are clean forgot,
    Gentlemen!

We have lost somewhat, afar and near.
    Gentlemen,
The thinning of our ranks each year
Affords a hint we are nigh undone,
That we shall not be ever again
The marked of many, loved of one,
    Gentlemen.

In dance the polka hit our wish,
    Gentlemen,
The paced quadrille, the spry schottische,
"Sir Roger."—And in opera spheres
The "Girl" (the famed "Bohemian"),
And "Trovatore," held the ears,
    Gentlemen.

This season's paintings do not please,
    Gentlemen,
Like Etty, Mulready, Maclise;
Throbbing romance has waned and wanned;
No wizard wields the witching pen
Of Bulwer, Scott, Dumas, and Sand,
    Gentlemen.

The bower we shrined to Tennyson,
    Gentlemen,
Is roof-wrecked; damps there drip upon
Sagged seats, the creeper-nails are rust,
The spider is sole denizen;
Even she who voiced those rhymes is dust,
    Gentlemen!

We who met sunrise sanguine-souled,
     Gentlemen,
Are wearing weary. We are old;
These younger press; we feel our rout
Is imminent to Aïdes' den,—
That evening shades are stretching out,
     Gentlemen!

And yet, though ours be failing frames,
     Gentlemen,
So were some others' history names,
Who trode their track light-limbed and fast
As these youth, and not alien
From enterprise, to their long last,
     Gentlemen.

Sophocles, Plato, Socrates,
     Gentlemen,
Pythagoras, Thucydides,
Herodotus, and Homer,—yea,
Clement, Augustin, Origen,
Burnt brightlier towards their setting-day,
     Gentlemen.

And ye, red-lipped and smooth-browed; list,
     Gentlemen;
Much is there waits you we have missed;
Much lore we leave you worth the knowing,
Much, much has lain outside our ken:
Nay, rush not: time serves: we are going,
     Gentlemen.

WAITING BOTH

A star looks down at me,
And says: "Here I and you
Stand, each in our degree.

What do you mean to do,—
    Mean to do?"

I say: "For all I know,
Wait, and let Time go by,
Till my change come,"—"Just so."
The star says: "So mean I:—
    So mean I."

IN ST. PAUL'S A WHILE AGO

Summer and winter close commune
On this July afternoon
As I enter chilly Paul's,
With its chasmal classic walls.
—Drifts of gray illumination
From the lofty fenestration
Slant them down in bristling spines that spread
Fan-like upon the vast dust-moted shade.

Moveless here, no whit allied
To the daemonian din outside,
Statues stand, cadaverous, wan,
Round the loiterers looking on
Under the yawning dome and nave,
Pondering whatnot, giddy or grave.
Here a verger moves a chair,
Or a red rope fixes there:—
A brimming Hebe, rapt in her adorning,
Brushes an Artemisia craped in mourning;

Beatrice Benedick piques, coquetting;
All unknowing or forgetting
That strange Jew, Damascus-bound,
Whose name, thereafter travelling round
To this precinct of the world,

Spread here like a flag unfurled:
Anon inspiring architectural sages
To frame this pile, writ his throughout the ages:
    Whence also the encircling mart
    Assumed his name, of him no part,
    And to his vision-seeing mind
    Charmless, blank in every kind;
And whose displays, even had they called his eye,
No gold or silver had been his to buy;

Whose haunters, had they seen him stand
On his own steps here, lift his hand
In stress of eager, stammering speech,
And his meaning chanced to reach,
Would have proclaimed him as they passed
An epilept enthusiast.

EVERY ARTEMISIA

"Your eye-light wanes with an ail of care,
Frets freeze gray your face and hair."

    "I was the woman who met him,
        Then cool and keen,
        Whiling away
Time, with its restless scene on scene
        Every day."

"Your features fashion as in a dream
Of things that were, or used to seem."

    "I was the woman who won him:
        Steadfast and fond
        Was he, while I
Tepidly took what he gave, nor conned
        Wherefore or why."

"Your house looks blistered by a curse,
As if a wraith ruled there, or worse."

"I was the woman who slighted him:
      Far from my town
      Into the night
He went. . . . My hair, then auburn-brown,
      Pangs have wanned white."

"Your ways reflect a monstrous gloom;
Your voice speaks from within a tomb."

"I was the woman who buried him:
      My misery
      God laughed to scorn:
The people said: ' 'Twere well if she
      Had not been born!' "

"You plod to pile a monument
So madly that your breath is spent."

"I am the woman who god him:
      I build, to ease
      My scalding fires,
A temple topping the Deities'
      Fanes of my sires."

THE BEST SHE COULD

Nine leaves a minute
Swim down shakily;
Each one fain would spin it
Straight to earth; but, see,
How the sharp airs win it
Slantwise away!—Hear it say,
"Now we have finished our summer show

Of what we knew the way to do:
Alas, not much! But, as things go,
As fair as any. And night-time calls,
    And the curtain falls!"

Sunlight goes on shining
As if no frost were here,
Blackbirds seem designing
Where to build next year;
    Yet is warmth declining:
And still the day seems to say,
"Saw you how Dame Summer drest?
Of all God taught her she bethought her!
Alas, not much! And yet the best
She could, within the too short time
    Granted her prime."

November 1923.

A NIGHT OF QUESTIONINGS

On the eve of All-Souls' Day
I heard the dead men say
Who lie by the tottering tower,
To the dark and doubling wind
At the midnight's turning hour,
When other speech had thinned:
    "What of the world now?"
The wind whiffed back: "Men still
Who are born, do good, do ill
Here, just as in your time:
Till their years the locust hath eaten,
Leaving them bare, downbeaten;
Somewhiles in springtide rime,
Somewhiles in summer glow,
Somewhiles in winter snow:—
    No more I know."

The same eve I caught cry
To the selfsame wind, those dry
As dust beneath the aisles
Of old cathedral piles.
Walled up in vaulted biers
Through many Christian years:
    "What of the world now?"
Sighed back the circuiteer:
"Men since your time, shrined here
By deserved ordinance,
Their own craft, or by chance,
Which follows men from birth
Even until under earth,
But little difference show
When ranged in sculptured row,
Different as dyes although:—
    No more I know."

On the selfsame eve, too, said
Those swayed in the sunk sea-bed
To the selfsame wind as it played
With the tide in the starless shade
From Comorin to Horn,
And round by Wrath forlorn:
    "What of the world now?"
And the wind for a second ceased,
Then whirred: "Men west and east,
As each sun soars and dips,
Go down to the sea in ships
As you went—hither and thither;
See the wonders of the deep,
As you did, ere they sleep;
But few at home care whither
They wander to and fro;
Themselves care little also!—
    No more I know."

Said, too, on the selfsame eve
The troubled skulls that heave
And fust in the flats of France,
To the wind wayfaring over
Listlessly as in trance
From the Ardennes to Dover,
    "What of the world now?"
And the farer moaned: "As when
You mauled these fields, do men
Set them with dark-drawn breaths
To knave their neighbours' deaths
In periodic spasms!
Yea, fooled by foul phantasms,
In a strange cyclic throe
Backward to type they go:—
    No more I know."

That night, too, men whose crimes
Had cut them off betimes,
Who lay within the pales
Of town and county jails
With the rope-groove on them yet,
Said to the same wind's fret
    "What of the world now?"
And the blast in its brooding tone
Returned: "Men have not shown,
Since you were stretched that morning,
A white cap your adorning,
More lovely deeds or true
Through thus neck-knotting you;
Or that they purer grow,
Or ever will, I trow!—
    No more I know."

LIFE AND DEATH AT SUNRISE

(NEAR DOGBURY GATE, 1867)

The hills uncap their tops
Of woodland, pasture, copse,
And look on the layers of mist
At their foot that still persist:
They are like awakened sleepers on one elbow lifted,
Who gaze around to learn if things during night have shifted.

A waggon creaks up from the fog
With a laboured leisurely jog;
Then a horseman from off the hill-tip
Comes clapping down into the dip;
While woodlarks, finches, sparrows, try to entune at one time,
And cocks and hens and cows and bulls take up the chime.

With a shouldered basket and flagon
A man meets the one with the waggon,
And both the men halt of long use.
"Well," the waggoner says, "what's the news?"
"—'Tis a boy this time. You've just met the doctor trotting back.
She's doing very well. And we think we shall call him 'Jack.'

"And what have you got covered there?"
He nods to the waggon and mare.
"Oh, a coffin for old John Thinn:
We are just going to put him in."
"—So he's gone at last. He always had a good constitution."
"—He was ninety-odd. He could call up the French Revolution."

A LIGHT SNOW-FALL AFTER FROST

On the flat road a man at last appears:
How much his whitening hairs
Owe to the settling snow's mute anchorage,

And how much to a life's rough pilgrimage,
    One cannot certify.

    The frost is on the wane,
And cobwebs hanging close outside the pane
Pose as festoons of thick white worsted there,
Of their pale presence no eye being aware
    Till the rime made them plain.

    A second man comes by;
His ruddy beard brings fire to the pallid scene:
    His coat is faded green;
    Hence seems it that his mien
    Wears something of the dye
Of the berried holm-trees that he passes nigh.

The snow-feathers so gently swoop that though
    But half an hour ago
The road was brown, and now is starkly white,
A watcher would have failed defining quite
    When it transformed it so.

Near Surbiton.

THE AËROLITE

I thought a germ of Consciousness
Escaped on an aërolite
        Aions ago
From some far globe, where no distress
Had means to mar supreme delight;

But only things abode that made
The power to feel a gift uncloyed
        Of gladsome glow,
And life unendingly displayed
Emotions loved, desired, enjoyed.

And that this stray, exotic germ
Fell wanderingly upon our sphere,
  After its wingings,
Quickened, and showed to us the worm
That gnaws vitalities native here,

And operated to unblind
Earth's old-established innocence
  Of stains and stingings,
Which grin no griefs while not opined
But cruelly tax intelligence.

"How shall we," then the seers said,
"Oust this awareness, this disease
  Called sense, here sown,
Though good, no doubt, where it was bred,
And wherein all things work to please?"

Others cried: "Nay, we rather would,
Since this untoward gift is sent
  For ends unknown,
Limit its registerings to good,
And hide from it all anguishment."

I left them pondering. This was how
(Or so I dreamed) was waked on earth
  The mortal moan
Begot of sentience. Maybe now
Normal unawareness waits rebirth.

"SHE OPENED THE DOOR"

She opened the door of the West to me,
  With its loud sea-lashings,
  And cliff-side clashings
Of waters rife with revelry.

She opened the door of Romance to me,
        The door from a cell
        I had known too well,
Too long, till then, and was fain to flee.

She opened the door of a Love to me,
        That passed the wry
        World-welters by
As far as the arching blue the lea.

She opens the door of the Past to me,
        Its magic lights,
        Its heavenly heights,
When forward little is to see!

        1913.

THE HARBOUR BRIDGE

From here, the quay, one looks above to mark
The bridge across the harbour, hanging dark
Against the day's-end sky, fair-green in glow
Over and under the middle archway's bow:
It draws its skeleton where the sun has set,
Yea, clear from cutwater to parapet;
On which mild glow, too, lines of rope and spar
        Trace themselves black as char.

Down here in shade we hear the painters shift
Against the bollards with a drowsy lift,
As moved by the incoming stealthy tide.
High up across the bridge the burghers glide
As cut black-paper portraits hastening on
In conversation none knows what upon:
Their sharp-edged lips move quickly word by word
        To speech that is not heard.

There trails the dreamful girl, who leans and stops,
There presses the practical woman to the shops,
There is a sailor, meeting his wife with a start,
And we, drawn nearer, judge they are keeping apart.
Both pause. She says: "I've looked for you. I thought
We'd make it up." Then no words can be caught.
At last: "Won't you come home?" She moves still nigher:
    " 'Tis comfortable, with a fire."

"No," he says gloomily. "And, anyhow,
I can't give up the other woman now:
You should have talked like that in former days,
When I was last home." They go different ways.
And the west dims, and yellow lamplights shine:
And soon above, like lamps more opaline,
White stars ghost forth, that care not for men's wives,
    Or any other lives.

    WEYMOUTH.

THE MISSED TRAIN

    How I was caught
Hieing home, after days of allure,
And forced to an inn—small, obscure—
    At the junction, gloom-fraught.

    How civil my face
To get them to chamber me there—
A roof I had scorned, scarce aware
    That it stood at the place.

    And how all the night
I had dreams of the unwitting cause
Of my lodgment. How lonely I was
    How consoled by her sprite!

Thus onetime to me. . . .
Dim wastes of dead years bar away
Then from now. But such happenings to-day
  Fall to lovers, may be!

Years, years as shoaled seas,
Truly, stretch now between! Less and less
Shrink the visions then vast in me.—Yes,
  Then in me: Now in these.

A POPULAR PERSONAGE AT HOME

"I live here: 'Wessex' is my name:
I am a dog known rather well:
I guard the house; but how that came
To be my whim I cannot tell.

"With a leap and a heart elate I go
At the end of an hour's expectancy
To take a walk of a mile or so
With the folk I let live here with me.

"Along the path, amid the grass
I sniff, and find out rarest smells
For rolling over as I pass
The open fields towards the dells.

"No doubt I shall always cross this sill,
And turn the corner, and stand steady,
Gazing back for my mistress till
She reaches where I have run already,

"And that this meadow with its brook,
And bulrush, even as it appears
As I plunge by with hasty look,
Will stay the same a thousand years."

Thus "Wessex." But a dubious ray
At times informs his steadfast eye,
Just for a trice, as though to say,
"Yet, will this pass, and pass shall I?"

"NOTHING MATTERS MUCH"

(B. F. L.)

"Nothing matters much," he said
Of something just befallen unduly:
He, then active, but now dead,
        Truly, truly!

He knew the letter of the law
As voiced by those of wig and gown,
Whose slightest syllogistic flaw
        He hammered down.

And often would he shape in word
That nothing needed much lamenting;
And she who sat there smiled and heard,
        Sadly assenting.

Facing the North Sea now he lies,
Toward the red altar of the East,
The Flamborough roar his psalmodies,
        The wind his priest.

And while I think of his bleak bed,
Of Time that builds, of Time that shatters,
Lost to all thought is he, who said
        "Nothing much matters."

THE SIX BOARDS

Six boards belong to me:
I do not know where they may be;
If growing green, or lying dry
    In a cockloft nigh.

Some morning I shall claim them,
And who may then possess will aim them
To bring to me those boards I need
    With thoughtful speed.

But though they hurry so
To yield me mine, I shall not know
How well my want they'll have supplied
    When notified.

Those boards and I—how much
In common we, of feel and touch
Shall share thence on,—earth's far core-quakings,
    Hill-shocks, tide-shakings—

Yea, hid where none will note,
The once live tree and man, remote
From mundane hurt as if on Venus, Mars,
    Or furthest stars.

"WHY DO I?"

Why do I go on doing these things?
    Why not cease?
Is it that you are yet in this world of welterings
    And unease,
And that, while so, mechanic repetitions please?

When shall I leave off doing these things?—
     When I hear
You have dropped your dusty cloak and taken you wondrous wings
     To another sphere,
Where no pain is: Then shall I hush this dinning gear.

THE NEW DAWN'S BUSINESS

What are you doing outside my walls,
     O Dawn of another day?
I have not called you over the edge
     Of the healthy ledge,
     So why do you come this way,
With your furtive footstep without sound here,
     And your face so deedily gray?

"I show a light for killing the man
     Who lives not far from you,
And for bringing to birth the lady's child,
     Nigh domiciled,
     And for earthing a corpse or two,
And for several other such odd jobs round here
     That Time to-day must do.

"But you he leaves alone (although,
     As you have often said,
You are always ready to pay the debt
     You don't forget
     You owe for board and bed):
The truth is, when men willing are found here
     He takes those loth instead."

DRINKING SONG

Once on a time when thought began
    Lived Thales: he
    Was said to see
Vast truths that mortals seldom can;
    It seems without
    A moment's doubt
That everything was made for man.

Chorus

Fill full your cups: feel no distress
That thoughts so great should now be less!

Earth mid the sky stood firm and flat,
    He held, till came
    A sage by name
Copernicus, and righted that.
    We trod, he told,
    A globe that rolled
Around a sun it warmed it at.

Chorus

Fill full your cups: feel no distress;
'Tis only one great thought the less!

But still we held, as Time flew by
    And wit increased,
    Ours was, at least,
The only world whose rank was high:
    Till rumours flew
    From folk who knew
Of globes galore about the sky.

Chorus

Fill full your cups: feel no distress;
'Tis only one great thought the less!

And that this earth, our one estate,
    Was no prime ball,
    The best of all,
But common, mean; indeed, tenth-rate:
    And men, so proud,
    A feeble crowd,
Unworthy any special fate.

Chorus

Fill full your cups: feel no distress;
'Tis only one great thought the less!

Then rose one Hume, who could not see,
    If earth were such,
    Required were much
To prove no miracles could be:
    "Better believe
    The eyes deceive
Than that God's clockwork jolts," said he.

Chorus

Fill full your cups: feel no distress;
'Tis only one great thought the less!

Next this strange message Darwin brings,
    (Though saying his say
    In a quiet way);
We all are one with creeping things;
    And apes and men
    Blood-brethren,
And likewise reptile forms with stings.

Chorus

Fill full your cups: feel no distress;
'Tis only one great thought the less!

And when this philosoph had done
    Came Doctor Cheyne:
    Speaking plain he
Proved no virgin bore a son.
    "Such tale, indeed,
    Helps not our creed,"
He said. "A tale long known to none."

Chorus

    Fill full your cups: feel no distress;
    'Tis only one great thought the less!

And now comes Einstein with a notion—
    Not yet quite clear
    To many here—
That's there's no time, no space, no motion,
    Nor rathe nor late,
    Nor square nor straight,
But just a sort of bending-ocean.

Chorus

    Fill full your cups: feel no distress;
    'Tis only one great thought the less!

So here we are, in piteous case:
    Like butterflies
    Of many dyes
Upon an Alpine glacier's face:
    To fly and cower
    In some warm bower
Our chief concern in such a place.

Chorus

    Fill full your cups: feel no distress;
    At all our great thoughts shrinking less:
    We'll do a good deed nevertheless!

NEW YEAR'S EVE*

Then he: "My labours—logicless—
    You may explain; not I:
Sense-sealed I have wrought, without a guess
That I evolved a Consciousness
    To ask for reasons why.

"Strange that ephemeral creatures who
    By my own ordering are,
Should see the shortness of my view,
Use ethic tests I never knew,
    Or made provision for!"

He sank to raptness as of yore,
    And opening New Year's Day
Wove it by rote as theretofore,
And went on working evermore
    In his unweeting way.

1906.

* Continued from page 37.

INDEX OF TITLES